VOLUME 7 ISSUE 4 **2007**

climate policy

integrating climate change actions into local development

Climate Policy is published 6 times a year by Earthscan, 2 Park Square, Milton Park, Abingdon, Oxfordshire OX14 4RN 711 Third Avenue, New York, NY 10017

First issued in paperback 2014

Earthscan is an imprint of the Taylor & Francis Group, an informa business

© 2007 Earthscan

ISBN 13: 978-1-84407-552-2 (hbk)
ISBN 13: 978-1-138-01221-9 (pbk)
ISSN: 1469-3062 (print), 1752-7457 (online)

Responsibility for statements made in the articles printed herein rests solely with the contributors. The views expressed by individual authors are not necessarily those of the editors, the funders or the publisher.

Climate Policy is editorially independent. The editorial administration of the journal is supported by Climate Strategies (a not-for-profit research network) and the region *Ile de France*.

Climate Policy is distributed by Portland Customer Services. Orders can be placed online at www.climatepolicy.com or sent to Portland Customer Services using the contact details below. Institutional subscriptions are £350/$630/€510 per volume (air mail extra); personal subscriptions are £99/$180/€145 per volume (air mail extra).

Post: Portland Customer Services,
         Commerce Way, Colchester,
         CO2 8HP, UK
Fax: +44 (0)1206 799331
Tel: +44 (0)1206 796351
Email: sales@portland-services.com

Abstracting and indexing services that cite *Climate Policy* include: ISI Social Sciences Citation Index and International Political Science Abstracts.

The Publishers acknowledge the generous support of Shell Foundation and Climate Strategies for the publication of this journal.

Climate Strategies

earthscan
from Routledge

Aims and scope

Climate Policy presents the highest quality refereed research and analysis on the policy issues raised by climate change, and provides a forum for commentary and debate. It addresses both the mitigation of, and adaptation to, climate change, within and between the different regions of the world. It encourages a trans-disciplinary approach to these issues at international, regional, national and sectoral levels.

The journal aims to make complex, policy-related analysis of climate change issues accessible to a wide audience, including those actors involved in:

- research and the commissioning of policy-relevant research
- policy and strategy formulation/implementation by local and national governments;
- the interactions and impacts of climate policies and strategies on business and society, and their responses, in different nations and sectors;
- international negotiations including, but not limited to, the UN Framework Convention on Climate Change, the Kyoto Protocol, other processes.

Climate Policy thus aims to build on its academic base so as to inject new insights and facilitate informed debate within and between, these diverse constituencies.

Types of contribution

Climate Policy publishes a variety of contributions:

Peer reviewed articles

Peer reviewed articles present academic, evidence-based research on climate policy issues:

- **Research articles** (4–6000 words) present original high quality research
- **Synthesis articles** (6–8000 words) present a survey and syntheses of the state of knowledge and key issues in a particular area of relevance to climate policy, including scientific, economic, environmental, institutional, political, social or ethical issues.
- **Policy analysis articles** (1–3000 words) present evidence-based objective analysis of policy that is embedded within an existing literature and context.

Research and synthesis articles are subject to rigorous double-blind multiple academic peer review; policy analysis articles are also fully peer-reviewed.

Outlook

The Outlook section presents timely, relevant analysis and commentary, for a wide climate policy community, and includes:

- **Perspectives** from senior decisionmakers
- **Insights** from independent commentators on policy processes, positions, options and debates
- **Records** of important new agreements, legislation and other developments including analysis of key events
- **Feedback** on earlier material published in *Climate Policy*

Climate Policy Outlook contains both commissioned and submitted papers, subject to editorial and light external review, generally in the range 500-2000 words though longer pieces may be considered on an exceptional basis.

Climate Policy also carries **country studies** and **book reviews**, and publishes **special thematic issues** on particular topics.

Topics covered

Topics covered by *Climate Policy* include (but are not limited to):

- Analysis of mitigation or adaptation policies and strategies (at macro-, meso- and/or micro- scales)
- Studies of implementation and prospects in different countries and industrial sectors
- Sectoral options and strategies for meeting policy targets
- Studies on regional differences including North-South issues
- Policy and economic aspects of intergenerational and intragenerational equity
- Applications of integrated assessment to specific policy issues
- Policy and quantitative aspects of land-use and forestry
- Design of the Kyoto mechanisms and their implications
- Analysis of corporate strategies for climate change
- Socio-political analysis of prospects for the UNFCCC system
- Economic and political aspects of developing country policy formation, action and involvement
- Social studies of climate change, including public perception, where policy implications are derived
- Local resilience, adaptation and insurance measures: extreme events and gradual change
- National and international adaptation and coping with impacts, including migration, natural resource allocation and use, etc.
- Policy formulation processes, including negotiation, public consultation, political processes and 'bottom-up' approaches

Authors' charter

This journal is committed to maintain the highest editorial standards and continuous improvement. As part of moving to an online submission system, we are implementing an Authors' Charter (see www.climatepolicy.com) to make our procedures and policies explicit and to help authors understand the editorial process and what to expect. As part of maintaining the highest standards, *Climate Policy* asks all authors, editors and reviewers to disclose any relationship (e.g. financial, economic or institutional) that could be perceived as affecting the integrity of the scientific process.

About the contributors

Livia Bizikova holds a fellowship of the Natural Sciences and Engineering Research Council of Canada (NSERC), working with the Adaptation and Impacts Research Division (AIRD) of Environment Canada and the W. Maurice Young Centre for Applied Ethics at the University of British Columbia. Livia's work focuses on the new initiative of AIRD, targeting linkages between climate change mitigation and adaptation and sustainable development (AMSD). This work includes organizing international workshops and three local case studies. She was also involved in the European study examining the cost of adaptation (European Environmental Agency) and in the development of adaptation capacity within the Integrated Vulnerability and Adaptation pilot project of the UNDP-GEF. Her PhD thesis examines the socio-economic impacts of land-use change and linkages with climate change in transition countries. She has participated in the Young Scientists Summer Programme at IIASA (Austria), and capacity-building initiatives of the International Human Dimension Programme (IHDP), and has gained Fellowships at Malardalen University (Sweden) and the University of Toronto (Canada).

Sarah Burch is exploring barriers to action in response to climate change at the municipal scale as part of the research programme of the Institute for Resources, Environment, and Sustainability at the University of British Columbia. She is a contributing author to chapters in both Working Group II (*Impacts, Adaptation and Vulnerability*) and Working Group III (*Mitigation of Climate Change*) of the Intergovernmental Panel on Climate Change's Fourth Assessment Report, and is investigating the effect of 3D computer-generated visualizations of local climate impacts and response options with UBC's Local Climate Change Visioning Project. She holds degrees in International Relations and Environmental Science, and is currently completing a PhD in Resource Management and Environmental Studies.

Ian Burton is Scientist Emeritus with the Adaptation and Impacts Research Division (AIRD) of the Meteorological Service of Canada, and Professor Emeritus at the University of Toronto. He was the founding director of AIRD and Director of the Institute of Environmental Studies at the University of Toronto. He is now also a Senior Visiting Fellow at the International Institute for Environment and Development in London. Other positions held include Senior Policy Advisor with Environment Canada, and Director of the International Federation of Institutes for Advanced Study. Ian has published widely on natural and man-made hazards and risk assessment; environment and development; water resources management; and climate change. He currently works mainly in the interface between science and policy and has contributed to IPCC Assessments and the work of the United Nations Framework Convention on Climate Change. Ian has served as consultant and advisor to many international and Canadian governmental agencies and engineering firms, and has worked for the Ford Foundation in India, Sudan and Nigeria. He has published several books and over 150 professional papers and is a Fellow of the Royal Society of Canada and the World Academy of Arts and Sciences.

Dana Coelho graduated with a dual Masters degree in Sustainable Development and Conservation Biology and Environmental Policy at the University of Maryland, where, until July 2007, she worked as a Research Associate at the Center for Integrative Environmental Research. She recently started as a Presidential Management Fellow in the Washington office of the US Forest Service Urban and Community Forestry Program.

Stewart J. Cohen is a Senior Researcher with the Adaptation and Impacts Research Division (AIRD), Environment Canada, and an Adjunct Professor with the Department of Forest Resources Management, University of British Columbia (UBC). Over a 25-year period, Stewart has authored more than 75 publications on climate change impacts and adaptation, and has organized case studies throughout Canada. His current activities include climate change visualization, and linking climate change and water management. He has contributed to several publications of the Intergovernmental Panel on Climate Change (IPCC), including the IPCC's Third and Fourth Assessment Reports, as well as the US Climate Change Science Program Synthesis and Assessment Product on *Weather and Climate Extremes in a Changing Climate*,

© 2007 Earthscan ISSN: 1469-3062 (print), 1752-7457 (online) www.climatepolicy.com

currently in review. He teaches a graduate course on Climate Change at UBC, and has been an adviser, reviewer and lecturer for various research and training programmes in North America, Europe and China. He obtained BSc, MSc and PhD degrees in Geography at McGill University, University of Alberta and University of Illinois, respectively.

Thea Dickinson is a Research Associate for the Adaptation and Impacts Research Division (AIRD) of Environment Canada, at Downsview, Ontario. She holds a Masters degree in Environmental Science from the University of Toronto (2006) and an Honours BSc in Applied Chemistry and Biology from Ryerson University (2005). Her studies have included soil contamination chemistry, boundary layer climates, and environmental risk assessment. Her most recent research project is the production of a compendium of adaptation models for climate change.

Siri Eriksen is a Post-doctoral Researcher in the Department of Sociology and Human Geography at the University of Oslo. She has a PhD in Environmental Sciences from the University of East Anglia. She has done research for the past 10 years on climate change and development, with particular attention paid to household-level vulnerability and adaptation to climate variability and change in Africa. Recent projects focus on the impact of conflict on vulnerability to climate change among dryland populations in Kenya; the effect of market integration on household responses to droughts and floods in Mozambique; and identifying critical linkages between adaptation and poverty reduction efforts in development policy. She has also studied vulnerability and adaptation to climate change in Norway. She has published extensively on climate change vulnerability and adaptation in Africa, and served as a reviewer of the Intergovernmental Panel on Climate Change's Fourth Assessment Report (2007).

Yvonne Howard is a Research Associate for the Adaptation and Impacts Research Division (AIRD) of Environment Canada, at Downsview, Ontario. She moved into climate change adaptation research after working for nearly 5 years in environmental education and wildlife conservation in both Ontario and British Columbia. With AIRD, Yvonne has provided research support for several adaptation projects. Her most recent research focus has been the collection and analysis of adaptation case studies in Canada. She holds a degree in Environmental Studies from the University of Toronto.

Tim McDaniels is a specialist in decision-making and risk management in environmental and infrastructure contexts. He is a Professor at the University of British Columbia, where he teaches in three graduate interdisciplinary programmes. He is also an Adjunct Professor in Engineering and Public Policy at Carnegie Mellon University. He has a special interest in multiple objective approaches to decision-making for risk management questions, and has experience in work with stakeholder advisory groups for complex environmental decisions. He has published over 40 refereed articles in top journals concerned with risk management and decision-making, often for environmental policy issues. He is a co-investigator in the Climate Decision Making Center at Carnegie Mellon University, and was formerly a co-investigator for 8 years at the Center for the Integrated Study of the Human Dimensions of Global Change. He has served as a member of national peer review and advisory committees for the Science Advisory Board of the US EPA, NOAA, NSF, and recently for the US National Academy of Sciences. He is a Fellow of the Society for Risk Analysis, has received the Society's distinguished service award, and is currently the Decision Sciences area editor for *Risk Analysis*. In 2003, he co-edited a new book published by Cambridge University Press, titled *Risk Analysis and Society*, which is a characterization of the state of the art and science of risk analysis for societal risk management choices.

Karen O'Brien is a Professor in the Department of Sociology and Human Geography at the University of Oslo, Norway, and Chair of the Global Environmental Change and Human Security (GECHS) project. She has been doing research related to climate change since 1988, and is currently interested in the relationship between climate change and human security, including the interactions between environmental change and globalization. She is presently leading a collaborative project on the Potentials of and Limits to Adaptation in Norway (PLAN), which investigates adaptation to climate change as a social process. Previous research has focused on assessments of climate change vulnerability and adaptive capacity at multiple scales in Norway; vulnerability to climate variability and trade liberalization in India; climate variability and the use of seasonal forecasts in southern Africa; and deforestation and climate change in southern Mexico. She is a lead author of the IPCC Fourth Assessment Report for Working Group II, and recently completed a book (co-authored with Robin Leichenko) entitled *Double Exposure: Global Environmental Change in an Era of Globalization* (Oxford University Press, 2008).

Rob Swart is Manager of the European Topic Centre for Air and Climate Change (ETC/ACC) of the European Environment Agency (EEA) at MNP (The Netherlands Environmental Assessment Agency). He has spent most of his career at the Dutch National Institute for Public Health and Environment (RIVM), focusing on integrated assessment of international environmental issues and scenario development. For shorter periods he has worked for the World Health Organization, the United States Environmental Protection Agency, the University of British Colombia, and the European Union's Joint Research Centre. He has been involved in all four IPCC Assessments, during the Third Assessment as Head of the Technical Support Unit of Working Group III on Mitigation and currently as a lead author of the WG III and the Synthesis Reports of the Fourth Assessment Report. His publications include many papers in scientific journals and a number of books, mostly on integrated assessment of climate change and sustainable development.

Frank Raes has been the Head of the Climate Change Unit at the European Commission's Joint Research Centre since 1989. He performed basic research on atmospheric aerosols while at the University of Ghent (Belgium) and the University of California of Los Angeles (USA). When entering the EC Joint Research Centre, he applied his knowledge to problems of air quality and climate change, and since then he and his team have been active in providing the scientific basis for developing integrated air quality and climate change policies. In parallel, he is also conducting research on the interface between science and policy-making, studying the similarities and differences between approaches under the UN Conventions on Long Range Transboundary Air Pollution and the UN Framework Convention on Climate Change.

John Robinson is a Professor with the Institute for Resources, Environment, and Sustainability, and the Department of Geography, at the University of British Columbia. He is currently directing research programmes looking at the intersection of climate change mitigation, adaptation and sustainability; the use of visualization, modelling and citizen engagement to explore sustainable futures; sustainable buildings and urban design; creating private/public/ NGO and research-sector partnerships for sustainability; and generally the intersection of sustainability, social and technological change, behaviour change, and community engagement processes. His major current project is trying to get the Centre for Interactive Research on Sustainability (CIRS) built and operating. He is a member of the Vancouver Climate Leadership Council, on the Board of the Sustainable Cities Foundation, a member of the Steering Group of HELIO International, and on the editorial boards of the journals *Integrated Assessment, Ecology and Society, Building Research and Information*, and the *Journal of Industrial Ecology*. He has been a lead author in the last three Reports of the Intergovernmental Panel on Climate Change.

Matthias Ruth is Roy F. Weston Chair in Natural Economics, Founding Director of the Center for Integrative Environmental Research at the Division of Research, Director of the Environmental Policy Program at the School of Public Policy, and Co-Director of the Engineering and Public Policy Program at the University of Maryland, USA, as well as a member of the faculty at the University of Bremen, Germany. His research focuses on dynamic modelling of natural resource use, industrial and infrastructure systems analysis, and environmental economics and policy. His theoretical work draws heavily on concepts from engineering, economics and ecology, while his applied research utilizes methods of non-linear dynamic modelling as well as adaptive and anticipatory management. Professor Ruth has published 10 books and over 100 papers and book chapters in the scientific literature. He collaborates extensively with scientists and policy-makers in the USA, Canada, Europe, Oceania, Asia and Africa.

Thomas J. Wilbanks has been a Corporate Research Fellow at the Oak Ridge National Laboratory since 1986 and leads the Laboratory's Global Change and Developing Country Programs. He conducts research on such issues as sustainable development, responses to environmental hazards and changes, and the role of geographical scale in these issues. Co-edited recent books include *Global Change and Local Places* (2003), *Geographical Dimensions of Terrorism* (2003), and *Bridging Scales and Knowledge Systems: Linking Global Science and Local Knowledge* (2006). Currently, he is serving as coordinating lead author for the IPCC's Fourth Assessment Report, Working Group II, Chapter 7: 'Industry, settlement, and society', and as a lead author of the Working Group II Technical Summary and Summary for Policymakers. He is also leading several 'synthesis and assessment' reports for the US Climate Change Science Program (CCSP), including summaries of current knowledge about impact and resilience issues for human settlements in the USA and for energy production and use in the USA. Thomas is a member of the

Board on Earth Sciences and Resources of the US National Research Council (NRC) and Chair of NRC's Standing Committee on Human Dimensions of Global Change, and he also serves on a number of other NRC committees and panels.

Charlie Wilson is an inter-disciplinary environmental researcher at the University of British Columbia. His current research concerns individual behaviour and decision-making and its consequences on energy use. Specifically he is testing the applicability of contrasting behavioural models to homeowners' decisions to undertake energy-efficient renovations, and to private developers' decisions to connect their buildings to a renewable district energy system. Complementing this descriptive behavioural research, he has also worked on prescriptive approaches to behaviour change using structured decision methods and backcasting/scenario analysis. Prior to moving to Canada, Charlie worked in the UK, most recently providing financial services for the renewable energy industry (mainly wind farms) and, before that, in an analytical role developing market-based policies for climate change mitigation.

climate
policy

■ editorial

Linking climate change and sustainable development at the local level

LIVIA BIZIKOVA[1]*, JOHN ROBINSON[2], STEWART COHEN[3]

[1] Adaptation and Impact Research Group (AIRG), Environment Canada and The Maurice Young Centre for Applied Ethics, The University of British Columbia, 6356 Agricultural Road, Vancouver, BC, V6T 1Z4, Canada
[2] Institute for Resources, Environment and Sustainability (IRES), University of British Columbia, 2202 Main Mall, Vancouver, BC, V6T 1Z4 Canada
[3] Adaptation and Impacts Research Division (AIRD), Environment Canada, Department of Forest Resources Management, Faculty of Forestry, University of British Columbia, 4617–2424 Main Mall, Vancouver, BC, V6T 1Z4 Canada

At continental and regional scales, numerous long-term changes in climate have already been observed, including changes in arctic temperatures and ice, widespread changes in precipitation amounts, wind patterns and aspects of extreme weather such as droughts, heavy precipitation, heatwaves and the intensity of tropical cyclones (IPCC, 2007a). The magnitude of observed impacts and anticipated future consequences of climate change has focused the attention of public and policy-makers not only on climate change adaptation and mitigation, but also on current notions of development. It is increasingly being recognized that climate change and development interact in a circular fashion (Downing et al., 2003). Specifically, climate change vulnerability and impacts influence prospects for development, and in turn, the development path not only determines greenhouse gas (GHG) emissions affecting future climate change, but also influences capacities to adapt and to mitigate climate change.

Although there is an empirical understating of the linkages between climate change and development, the bulk of current research discusses these linkages at the theoretical level without providing venues for their implementation. This special issue explores potential venues for integrating adaptation and mitigation within a development context, particularly at the local–regional levels. It is targeted towards scientists and policy-makers searching for innovative bottom-up approaches building on increasing local concerns about climate change. It seems that regional- and local-scale actions could provide a rich array of examples and best practices to interpret, guide and implement larger-scale initiatives including strategies for post-Kyoto 2012.

This special issue examines the questions of how to integrate adaptation and mitigation within a development context, particularly at the local–regional levels. As described below, the issues of policy formation, decision-making, governance and behavioural change require a focus at the local level if substantive progress is to be achieved. In particular, this Issue will present suggestions on how to include sustainable development thinking and policy in order to assist with the creation of local implementation pathways to increase the opportunities and capacity for effective mitigation and adaptation. In many communities, the principles of participation, social learning

■ *Corresponding author. E-mail: liviab@interchange.ubc.ca

© 2007 Earthscan ISSN: 1469-3062 (print), 1752-7457 (online) www.climatepolicy.com

and scenario development will be vital for successful implementation of adaptive, mitigative and sustainable development approaches. In addition, the policy focus needs to shift away from an exclusive concentration on environmental and climate change policies to embrace a broader set of tools, processes and policies.

Milestones in research addressing climate change and sustainability

In 1992, Article 2 of the United Nations Framework Convention on Climate Change (UNFCCC) emphasized the stabilization of GHG concentrations at levels allowing natural adaptation of ecosystems, and ensuring food security and sustainable economic development (UN, 1992). Some light on the relationship between development and climate change was shed by the IPCC SRES and post-SRES analyses,[1] which showed a significant impact of the development path on emissions, concentrations of GHG, and consequently on the magnitude of needed adaptation and mitigation responses. In particular, scenario families with an emphasis on global (B1) and local (B2) sustainability led to the lowest level of CO_2 concentrations and highest level of adaptive capacity, and consequently to higher resilience compared with the rest of the scenarios (Swart et al., 2003).

Since the publication of these results in 2000 and 2001, a growing literature has emerged that examines the relationship between climate change and sustainable development. This literature is mainly focused on analysing low-emission and clean energy pathways, mainstreaming climate change into development efforts in developing countries, and suggesting frameworks of integrated models to analyse these linkages (for example, Markandya and Halnaes, 2002; Metz et al., 2002; Winkler et al., 2002; Wilbanks, 2003).

In 2003, the *Climate Policy* special supplement on 'Climate Change and Sustainable Development' (Munasinghe and Downing, 2003) synthesized many of the latest developments in this area. This supplement identified two distinct approaches to climate change and sustainable development: integrating sustainable development into climate change policies and *vice versa* (Cohen et al., 1998; Swart et al., 2003) and presented an actual case study showing synergies between climate change responses and sustainable development in Vietnam (Dang et al., 2003). In their Editorial, Downing et al. (2003) emphasized the importance of conducting innovative assessments at the local and regional scales to address 'real vulnerabilities' by an involvement of stakeholders to help integrate values and economic reasoning within adaptation and mitigation actions.

Since then, the IPCC Fourth Assessment has identified the linkages between climate change and sustainable development, and between adaptation and mitigation as crosscutting themes across the Working Group II and III Reports. The recently published Working Group II 'Summary for policymakers' (IPCC, 2007b) stresses the importance of sustainable development in reducing vulnerability to climate change, as well as the role of climate in impeding nations' abilities to achieve sustainable development. However, it also states that only a few plans and cases promoting sustainability explicitly included climate change.

A recently published special issue of *Mitigation and Adaptation Strategies for Global Change* lists a number of examples of potential and actually implemented linkages between adaptation and mitigation in various sectors, including forestry, agriculture, water and insurance. The syntheses (Wilbanks and Sathaye, 2007) and other papers in the issue (Bhandari et al., 2007; Golkany, 2007) conclude that, with respect to promoting integrated adaptation and mitigation measures, the focus should be on sustainable development to provide a context for a mixture of adaptation and mitigation, depending on the magnitude and rate of climate change in particular local contexts. It recognizes a need for developing local capacities to enable realistic implementation pathways, and in this way to increase the chances in coping with progressing climate change.

Climate change and sustainable development at the local level

Expanding on this rich body of knowledge generated during recent years, this special issue of *Climate Policy* takes the research further by exploring an integrated approach considering the linkages among climate change adaptation (A) and mitigation (M) in the context of sustainable development (SD), which we refer to as AMSD. AMSD puts sustainable development first in recognition of the importance of development pathways on the level of emissions, available capacities, and character of actual responses to climate change. Like Wilbanks and Sathaye (2007), we emphasize that the linkages between adaptation and mitigation are highly context-specific and place-based depending on the priorities guiding development. In this way, AMSD emphasizes that climate change adaptation and mitigation are a part of the wider development goals in transition towards sustainability. Moreover, the effectiveness of adaptation and mitigation measures on their own is limited, especially those that aim for behavioural changes without challenging the underlying development pathway.

AMSD is built around principles of participation, scenario development, and social learning; and will be applied in local case studies in British Columbia and Ontario, Canada. The AMSD approach, for instance, suggests a participatory process that includes the following four stages: identifying a local sustainable development scenario, explicitly linking climate change impacts, identifying linkages between adaptation and mitigation, and developing an integrated AMSD implementation strategy. The process is iterative in order to incorporate the learning experiences of the gradual inclusion of climate change impacts, and the linkages between adaptation and mitigation measures and the local sustainability vision. At each stage of the process, we distinguish a number of methods including backcasting, trade-off analyses, strategy building, and number of participatory activities including local development goal selection, involving local knowledge in describing local systems, interpreting climate change impacts, and creating institutional partnerships (Bizikova et al., 2007).

Conducting local studies targeting sustainable development first, and then linking to climate change, raises complex issues. Such local studies will probably enhance interdisciplinary approaches; however, they will require robust data and information at a relatively small scale, and will rely heavily on multi-sector partnerships developed in an explicitly participatory process. Although we are optimistic regarding the potential value of participatory processes, it is important to recognize some concerns related to the application of these methods, including difficulties in engaging participants due to the considerable time requirements involved, and in adding to the pressure already being felt by local-scale decision-makers as national and international initiatives are downloaded onto their jurisdictions. We believe that interest in participation can be enhanced by creating opportunities for participants to be involved in setting up the overall research agenda and in fostering increases in their participatory capacities through shared learning exercises.

Focus of this special issue

The articles in this issue explore the integration of adaptation and mitigation responses, and capacities at the local development context by addressing three crucial questions that interact directly and indirectly with policy formation and execution, decision-making and governance:

1. From the local perspective, how do key synergies and trade-offs affect different responses to climate change involving adaptation and mitigation? And how could an integrated approach support local-scale actions rather than discouraging them?

2. What would such responses imply in terms of the capacities required to reduce vulnerability as a part of the local development pathways based on the principles of sustainable development?
3. What methodological approaches exist that would help to achieve both mitigation and adaptation responses to climate change embedded in the context of local sustainable development?

Focusing on a sustainable development perspective, Thomas Wilbanks' article focuses on navigating through 'the trajectory of change' towards local sustainability with explicit responses to climate change. This requires exploring the opportunities that resulted from combining the strengths of local, national and even global scales, and also developing linkages to deliver the experiences and knowledge from higher scales to the local level. Because each scale offers different types of opportunities for AMSD cases, Rob Swart and Frank Raes propose linking adaptation and mitigation at an early stage of development initiatives in order to identify these opportunities in the context of particular projects. To facilitate the shared adaptation and mitigation actions, both articles emphasize the need to create institutional partnerships that will provide venues to mainstream the identified responses from diverse scales into development initiatives.

Sarah Burch and John Robinson address the challenges of exploring the linkages between responses to climate change and development by reframing the very similar, yet separate, concepts of adaptive and mitigative capacities, and by developing the idea of response capacity. Response capacity represents a broader pool of development-related resources from which adaptive and mitigative capacities, and actual actions, are derived. Additionally, they are themselves embedded in socio-economic and technological development pathways. Beyond available capacities, however, Ian Burton et al. stress the role of international policy development, and its guiding principles of transforming capacities to actual mitigation and adaptation actions. This suggests that distinguishing between adaptation and mitigation is a rather artificial dichotomy reflecting the state of research at the time of the negotiation of the UN Framework Convention. It argues in favour of viewing the responses to climate change as deeply rooted in society. Consequently, these cannot be addressed without sufficient linkages to the responses of societal development needs.

To help operationalize the AMSD approach, we present case studies that link both types of responses within the development context. Focused on urban infrastructure, Matthias Ruth and Dana Coelho discuss a role of scenarios and strategies that are robust enough to capture future development paths, and to foster adaptive and anticipatory management options. Finally, in the case study from Kenya, Siri Eriksen and Karen O'Brien discuss the responses to climate change that are needed in order to reduce vulnerability as well as to improve development status at the local level. Their article stresses the presence of considerable differences between vulnerability and poverty reduction measures, and suggests that attention should be given to expanding narrowly defined methods for reducing biophysical risks towards policies aiming for sustainable development.

To move from the realm of identified responses to actual policies, Charlie Wilson and Tim McDaniels apply the principles of structural decision-making to support the AMSD decisions operating on multiple temporal and spatial scales, and multiple scales of governance. They see AMSD decisions as an outcome of pluralistic decision processes, often involving civil society through explicit stakeholder involvement.

Policy implications and conclusions

This broad array of articles identifies a number of challenges in integrating the diversity of actors, scales, sectors and governance structures that seem to be necessary to 'fit together' in order to benefit from the proposed AMSD approach. A local and regional focus is required to create concrete alternatives and directions within given development pathways. These individual small-scale actions could create a rich basis of examples to push the actions at national and global scales. In fact, effective actions at larger scales tend to be limited without these bottom-up encouragements. Larger-scale actions are then shaped and fine-tuned in association with smaller-scale stakeholders and, in fact, in large part implemented through smaller-scale actions (Burton et al.; Wilbanks).

In order to advance interconnected adaptation and mitigation capacities and responses to climate change within the context of sustainable development, a number of methodological challenges are identified in this issue. These include actions to:

1. *Enhance multidisciplinary assessments in developing complex policies.* These need to address climate change by accounting for the underlying development values and principles of applied models and assessment tools. This involves balancing the focus, especially in adaptation from biophysical risks associated with climate change and in mitigation from narrowly-defined sectoral GHG reduction policies, with the specific risks and opportunities to address issues such as well-being, response capacity, and processes shaping vulnerability (Eriksen and O'Brien).
2. *Expand participatory integrated assessment to built models.* This should facilitate the involvement of stakeholders in defining the course of development pathways, and create a context for the linkages between adaptation and mitigation by linking impacts and vulnerability to climate change with effectiveness of mitigation efforts (Ruth and Coelho).
3. *Elaborate the linkages between adaptation and mitigation capacities and actions.* This entails analysing the diversity of their dimensions, including social, economic, institutional, technological and cultural characteristics; and identifying shared areas, connections, and consequently potential reinforcements between adaptation and mitigation strategies (Burch and Robinson; Swart and Raes).
4. *Develop methodologies to assess trade-offs between adaptation and mitigation in respect of uncertainties within climate scenarios.* In this context, diversity of values and development priorities create support for actions and policies (Burton et al.; Wilson and McDaniels).
5. *Promote two-way communication in defining projects and disseminating results in collaboration with stakeholders.* This should be an explicit objective of the research projects.

Regardless of any significant remaining research gaps, the urgency of climate change calls for prompt decision outcomes. Policy-makers at the local level are in the difficult situation of trying to reconcile a wide diversity of local development visions with trade-offs over limited resources, at a time when more actions, both in mitigation and adaptation, will be needed in order to tackle future climate change impacts, as well as to protect us from climate-related surprises. Therefore, viewing adaptation and mitigation as separate fields of action and policy without direct linkages may work against the implementation of opportunities that are perhaps not the most significant contribution to emission reduction, or avoided climate damage, but which can still offer tangible local benefits. Such local actions may:

1. *Include climate change impacts in the local development planning process.* An AMSD approach has implications for much more than climate or environmental policy. Local taxes, infrastructure investments, land-use regulations and budget planning processes all have major implications for local or regional development paths and thus for adaptation and mitigation options and impacts. The local context frames the linkages between adaptation

and mitigation, and therefore the policy mix of adaptation and mitigation will differ from place to place.

2. *Evaluate socio-economic scenarios currently utilized in the local planning processes, and develop new scenarios as needed.* This is needed in order to uncover underlying principles directing the development trajectory that can be used to guide long-term development policies, including infrastructure and natural resource management in the community.

3. *Pay attention to diverse levels of capacity and vulnerability to climate change within the community, while developing adaptation and mitigation strategies.* Specifically, this means including those with a low level of adaptive capacity in capacity-building activities in order to lower their vulnerabilities and to create opportunities for them to be part of the solution.

4. *Develop linkages between the diversity of institutions focused on climate change adaptation, mitigation, and development at the local level.* This will help identify synergies between their institutional actions, promote networking, and foster communication, and in this way create opportunities to minimize trade-offs of narrowly focused development actions and response to climate change.

5. *Identify institutional partners at regional, national and international level in development of integrated responses to climate change.* This will promote knowledge-sharing from a diversity of cases in order to develop innovative links between development and climate change and provide guidelines for policy-makers working on the larger scale on how to inject development to climate change and *vice versa*.

6. *Approach universities, research institutions and local experts to develop shared projects to meet identified research needs while addressing local climate policy needs.* Collaboration with local practitioners is vital to create case studies, and reap the benefits of mutual learning.

Acknowledgements

We thank the contributors and the reviewers of the articles for this special issue. We also gratefully acknowledge the continuous support of the Adaptation and Impacts Research Division of Environment Canada for the International Workshop on AMSD Linkages in Vancouver, Canada (April 2006) which initiated the collaborative effort on AMSD, including our current case studies. We are also grateful to our colleagues at the University of British Columbia for their contributions, and engagement in the AMSD initiative.

Note

1. SRES emissions scenarios are scenarios of the IPCC Special Report on Emissions Scenarios (SRES) and post-SRES scenarios are modified versions of the SRES marker scenarios such that CO_2 concentrations are stabilized early in the 22nd century (Nakicenovic and Swart, 2000; Schlesinger and Malyshev, 2001; Metz et al., 2002).

References

Bhandari, P.M., Bhadwal, S., Kelkar, U., 2007, 'Examining adaptation and mitigation opportunities in the context of the integrated watershed management programme of the Government of India', *Mitigation and Adaptation Strategies for Global Change* 12, 919–933.

Bizikova, L., Burch, S., Cohen, S., Robinson, J., 2007, 'Climate change and sustainable development in the local context: linking research with local opportunities and challenges', *Global Environmental Change*, under review.

Burch, S., Robinson, J., 2007, 'A framework for explaining the links between capacity and action in response to global climate change', *Climate Policy* 7(4), 304–316.

Burton, I., Bizikova, L., Dickinson, T., Howard, Y., 2007, 'Integrating adaptation into policy: upscaling evidence from local to global', *Climate Policy* 7(4), 371–376.

Cohen, S., Demeritt, D., Robinson, J., Rothman, D., 1998, 'Climate change and sustainable development: towards dialogue', *Global Environmental Change* 8, 341–371.

Dang, H.H., Michaelowa, A., Tuan, D.D., 2003, 'Synergy of adaptation and mitigation strategies in the context of sustainable development: the case of Vietnam', *Climate Policy* 3(S1), S81–S96.

Downing, T.E., Munasinghe, M., Depledge, J., 2003, 'Special Supplement on Climate Change and Sustainable Development', *Climate Policy* 3(S1), S3–S8.

Eriksen, S., O'Brien, K. 2007, 'Vulnerability, poverty and the need for sustainable adaptation measures', *Climate Policy* 7(4), 337–352.

Golkany, I., 2007, Integrating strategies to reduce vulnerability and advance adaptation, mitigation and sustainable development. *Mitigation and Adaptation Strategies for Global Change* 12, 755–786.

IPCC, 2007a, 'Summary for policymakers', in: S. Solomon, D. Qin, M. Manning, Z. Chen, M. Marquis, K.B. Averyt, M. Tignor, H.L. Miller (eds), *Climate Change 2007: The Physical Science Basis. Contribution of Working Group I to the Fourth Assessment Report of the Intergovernmental Panel on Climate Change*, Cambridge University Press, Cambridge, UK.

IPCC, 2007b, 'Summary for policymakers', in: M.L. Parry, O.F. Canziani, J.P. Palutikof, P.J. van der Linden and C.E. Hanson (eds), *Climate Change 2007: Impacts, Adaptation and Vulnerability. Contribution of Working Group II to the Fourth Assessment Report of the Intergovernmental Panel on Climate Change*, Cambridge University Press, Cambridge, UK, 7–22.

Markandya, A., Halsneas K. (eds), 2002, *Climate Change and Sustainable Development*, Earthscan, London.

Metz, B., Berk, M., den Elzen, M., de Vries, B., van Vuuren, D., 2002, 'Towards an equitable climate change regime: compatibility with Article 2 of the Climate Change Convention and the link with sustainable development', *Climate Policy* 2, 211–230.

Munasinghe, M., Downing, T.E. (eds), 2003, *Special Supplement on Climate Change and Sustainable Development*, *Climate Policy*, 3, Supplement 1.

Nakicenovic, N., Swart, R.J. (eds), 2000, *IPCC Special Report on Emissions Scenarios*, Cambridge University Press, Cambridge, UK.

Ruth, M., Coelho, D. 2007, 'Understanding and managing the complexity of urban systems under climate change', *Climate Policy* 7(4), 317–336.

Schlesinger, M.E., Malyshev, S., 2001, 'Changes in near-surface temperature and sea level for the Post-SRES CO_2-stabilization scenarios', *Integrated Assessment* 2, 95–110.

Swart, R., Raes, F., 2007, 'Making integration of adaptation and mitigation work: mainstreaming into sustainable development policies?', *Climate Policy* 7(4), 288–303.

Swart, R., Robinson, J., Cohen, S., 2003, 'Climate change and sustainable development: expanding the options', *Climate Policy* 3(S1), S19–S40.

UN (United Nations), 1992, *United Nations Framework Convention on Climate Change*, FCCC/Informal/84 GE.05-62220 (E) 200705 [available at http://unfccc.int/resource/docs/convkp/conveng.pdf].

Wilbanks, T.J., 2003, 'Integrating climate change and sustainable development in a place-based context', *Climate Policy* 3(S1), S147–S154.

Wilbanks, T.J., 2007, 'Scale and sustainability', *Climate Policy* 7(4), 278–287.

Wilbanks, T.J., Sathaye, J., 2007, 'Integrating mitigation and adaptation as responses to climate change: a synthesis', *Mitigation and Adaptation Strategies for Global Change* 12, 957–962.

Winkler, H., Spalding-Fecher, R., Mwakasonda, S., Davidson, O., 2002, 'Sustainable development policies and measures: starting from development to tackle climate change', in: K.A. Baumert, O. Blanchard, S. Llosa, J. Perkaus (eds), *Building on the Kyoto Protocol: Options for Protecting the Climate*, World Resources Institute, Washington, DC.

Wilson, C., McDaniels, T., 2007, 'Structured decision-making to link climate change and sustainable development', *Climate Policy* 7(4), 353–370.

■ synthesis article

Scale and sustainability

THOMAS J. WILBANKS*

Oak Ridge National Laboratory, Oak Ridge, TN 37831-6038, USA

Geographical scale is a factor in interactions between climate change and sustainable development, because of varying spatial dynamics of key processes and because of varying scales at which decision-making is focused. In a world where the meaning of 'global' and 'local' is being reshaped by technological and social change, a challenge to sustainable development is realizing the impressive, but often elusive, potentials for climate-change-related actions at different scales to be complementary and reinforcing. Climate change adaptation is suggested as an example.

Keywords: adaptation; bottom-up; cross-scale; governance; multi-scale; scale; sustainability actions; sustainable development; top-down

L'échelle géographique est un facteur dans l'interaction entre changement climatique et développement durable, étant donnés les différentes échelles spatiales encadrant les processus clés et la prise de décisions focalisée à différentes échelles. Dans un monde où le sens des mots «mondial» et «local» est redéfini par les changements technologiques et sociaux, un enjeu relatif au développement durable est de réaliser le potentiel prodigieux mais souvent insaisissable de complémentarité et de synergie des actions la lutte contre le changement climatique applicables à différentes échelles. L'adaptation au changement climatique est proposé en tant qu'exemple.

Mots clés: actions durables; adaptation; bottom-up; développement durable; échelle; gouvernance; inter-échelle; multi-échelle; top-down

1. Introduction

Interactions between climate change and sustainable development are expressions of an ever-changing dance that happens at a variety of geographical scales, and appreciating this dance is one of the keys in assuring that sustainability can be realized.

This article considers how geographical scale is a factor in climate change/sustainable development interactions, especially in determining what kinds of actions are best focused on which scales and how actions at different scales may affect each other. First, it summarizes the conceptual starting points in a world in which the meanings of such constructs as 'global' and 'local' are being reshaped by technology and other forces of change. Next, it addresses ways in which scale is an aspect of sustainability, with brief examples. It then focuses on ways in which scale relates to sustainability actions. Finally, it turns to potentials for making climate-change-related sustainability actions at different geographical scales complementary and reinforcing, rather than unrelated or even in conflict, using climate change adaptation as an example.

■ *E-mail*: wilbankstj@ornl.gov

CLIMATE POLICY **7 (2007) 278–287**

2. Conceptual foundations

For the purposes of this article, geographical scale is defined as the spatial dimensions of a process, an observation, or a decision (see Capistrano et al., 2003). Sustainable development is defined as development that meets the social and economic needs of the world's population, current and future, without endangering the viability of environmental systems important to meeting those needs. In many cases, however, current understandings about relationships between scale and sustainable development are rather similar even if the definitions vary to some degree.

Scale can be viewed as a continuum between micro (very small) and macro (very large) (Meyer et al., 1992), but in practice the processes that drive and shape sustainability tend to organize themselves more characteristically at some scales than others, giving the sustainability scale continuum a kind of lumpiness (Wilbanks, 2003a). In many cases, reflecting this lumpiness, scales related to particular levels of system activity can be represented as mosaics of 'regions', each reflecting a characteristic scale, with smaller-scale mosaics apparently nested within larger-scale mosaics (Costanza et al., 2000) – which tends to invite speculations about spatial hierarchies, whether relevant to process relationships or not.

Geographical scale, of course, is not the only kind of scale important for sustainability (Cash et al., 2006). For instance, along with scales (or 'levels') of organizational structure, scale is a factor in time as well. Drawing on the literature in such fields as ecology, there has been a tendency to associate spatial and temporal scale: e.g. suggesting that sustainability-relevant time-scales in larger geographical areas are longer, while time-scales in smaller geographical areas are shorter (Capistrano et al., 2003), although many exceptions can be noted (such as the time horizons of some elected officials at national scales).

In any case, appreciating the roles of geographical scale for sustainability is profoundly complicated by constant changes in the world around us, especially as technologies reshape the meaning of proximity and increase interconnections over what were once long distances (Wilbanks, 2003b), often speeding the diffusion of innovations. Some alternatives for interaction appear to be released from distance constraints by technologies (and associated cultural changes) such as cyberspace.

Observers of global processes see a 'shrinking' globe, as distant neighbours become nearer neighbours (e.g., Harvey, 1989). Observers of local processes see areas in a mosaic being transcended by nodes in networks, as individual contact networks become less dominated by geographical proximity. Meanwhile, technology is changing the character of places by shaping what happens there, and it changes social demands for nature's services and tools for environmental management (Wilbanks, 2003b).

This suggests that familiar conceptions of *physical* scale are, at least in many parts of the developed world, evolving into a kind of *virtual* scale, which is changing the meaning of scale, location and locality in ways that are not yet fully understood.

3. Scale as an aspect of sustainability

Scale is an aspect of sustainability in that sustainable development involves differences between scales in systems and processes, understandings of issues, and abilities to act; relationships between scales in systems and processes, and in shaping each other's perceived realities and one's ability to act; and potentials for multi-scale analyses and actions (Wilbanks, 2003a; Kates and Wilbanks, 2003; Purvis and Grainger, 2004).

We know, for example, that sustainability in a neighbourhood is different from sustainability in a nation, and we know that sustainability in a localized ecology is different from sustainability in a regional ecosystem (Holling, 1995). We also know that what happens with sustainability at one scale affects sustainability at other scales. For instance, the subglobal component of the Millennium Ecosystem Assessment reported that, in some parts of the world, local situations are not sustainable while their larger regional situations appear to be relatively stable; while, in other parts of the world, local situations are quite stable while their larger regional situations appear to be in a state of crisis (Millennium Ecosystem Assessment, 2005).

A part of the explanation for this divergence in perceptions – and realities – is that sustainability may be viewed differently at different scales, and relevant information may not be the same (Rebozatti, 1993; Wilbanks and Kates, 1999). In many cases, for instance, there are differences between scales in complexity and in vulnerability (Eriksen and O'Brien, 2007). Smaller scales exhibit less complexity but, as a result, are more tractable in tracing out relationships in all their richness, while larger scales include more complexity but can only be addressed by simplifying the relationships in order to make analysis and understanding manageable (Kates et al., 2001). Regarding vulnerability (e.g. to severe weather events due to climate change), smaller scales have a lower probability of threat but less resilience if that threat were to be realized, while larger scales have a higher probability of threat somewhere within them but more resilience in coping with the threat, because as a general principle they have access to a wider range of resources for damage response and cost-sharing.

The different scales, however, are not independent of each other. As Figure 1 indicates, processes and actions at scales from local to global interact constantly, and these interactions

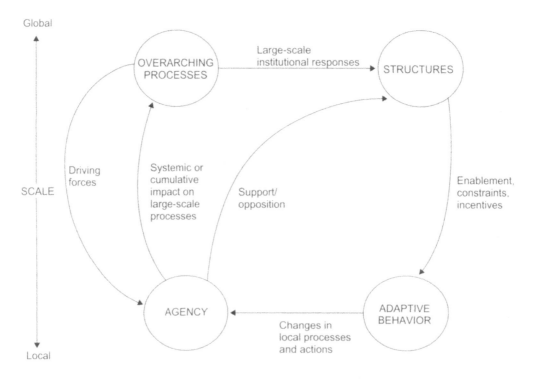

MACROSCALE/MICROSCALE INTERACTIONS IN GLOBAL CHANGE

FIGURE 1 Macroscale/microscale interactions in global change. Adapted from Wilbanks (2003a)

can pose a number of challenges to sustainability (Cash et al., 2006; Wilbanks et al., 2007a). Top-down forces can threaten an insensitivity to local contexts, a backlash from disenfranchised local stakeholders, and a lack of empowerment of local creativity. Bottom-up forces can threaten an accumulation of relatively small changes that add up to very large changes (Turner et al., 1990), a lack of sensitivity to larger-scale driving forces and issues, a lack of information about linkages between places and scales, and a lack of access to resources to support effective actions.

The fact is that sustainability is not a state; it is a trajectory of change (Wilbanks, 1994), depending on constant adjustments to both internal and external driving forces, both of which are subject to sometimes spontaneous and sometimes unpredictable changes, from technological innovation and socio-political leadership to biological mutation. In this regard, not all localities are shaped by every change at a larger scale; and not every large-scale system is affected by every change in every locality. But sustainability in any one place is to some degree threatened by a lack of sustainability in any other place, because ripple effects from non-sustainable circumstances can have far-reaching implications, from environmental migration to resource scarcity to roots of terrorism (Cutter et al., 2003).

Scale is also a factor in how we view and learn about sustainability (Wilbanks and Kates, 1999; AAG, 2003; Kates and Wilbanks, 2003). Sustainability is a challenge in multidisciplinary integration, and a major finding of sustainability studies over the past several decades is that such integration is most feasible if it is place-based (NAS, 1999; Kates et al., 2001; Wilbanks, 2003c). In many cases, it appears that responses to sustainability challenges that effectively integrate understandings of both natural and human systems, such as potentials for adaptation to climate change, depend heavily on locationally specific contexts, options, and avenues for action (Burch and Robinson, 2007).

Moreover, sustainability issues may appear different according to whether they are examined top-down or bottom-up. For instance, top-down analyses are strongly shaped by input assumptions that may not be appropriate for every locality, while bottom-up analyses can be so case-specific that extracting general lessons is difficult (Wilbanks, 2005; Wilbanks et al., 2007a).

Illustrations of scale as an aspect of sustainability are all around us. For instance, population growth is a global-scale driving force, but many of its implications are highly localized: e.g. historically, pressures in mainland Southeast Asia to make the painfully difficult socio-political transition from shifting agriculture to wet rice cultivation or, more recently, issues of equity in connection with larger-scale requirements for waste disposal in order to support economic growth.

Imbalances in the global carbon cycle, of which climate change is the most salient effect, are rooted in every aspect of scale relationships in our planet's coupled nature–society systems, as depicted in Figure 1. Global driving forces such as population and economic growth and technological change pour down upon localities hungry for opportunities and newly aware of alternatives as the information technology revolution spreads. Local actions seeking new comforts, conveniences, mobility and job opportunities – in the context of these driving forces – produce carbon emissions that add up to rising total emission curves. The resulting increases in radiative forcing at a global scale feed back downward as changes in climate and associated impacts on temperature, precipitation, extreme weather events, and the sea level. Impacts (or concerns about impacts) at local and regional scales join together to push for actions at national and global scales; in fact, without such bottom-up encouragement, effective actions by larger scales tend to be limited in democratic systems of government. Larger-scale actions are then shaped and fine-tuned in association with smaller-scale stakeholders and, in fact, in large part implemented through smaller-scale actions, whether related to carbon emission source reductions or sink enhancements (Burton et al., 2007). If the results are not sufficient to address imbalances and associated impacts, the process iterates further.

4. Scale and sustainability actions

Often, views of the relevance of scale in sustainability actions have reflected different academic disciplinary perspectives, e.g. political scientists interested in global-scale governance structures contrasting with cultural anthropologists interested in local-scale knowledge (Cash et al., 2006; Reid et al., 2006a). A challenge has been to find ways to knit these perspectives together to combine the insights of all (Reid et al., 2006b).

Several things are known at a relatively high level of confidence.

1. We know that decision-making based on broad societal participation requires personal interaction. There is abundant evidence that many decisions are shaped by personal communications, which relate to what has been called a 'choreography' of human interaction (Parkes and Thrift, 1980; after Hagerstrand, 1975). Where those personal interactions benefit from physical proximity, there tend to be physical limits to the social and spatial scale at which consensus or accommodation can be reached for some purposes. Clearly, proximity contributes to decision-making as a social process, connecting with such issues as empowerment, constituency-building and public participation. In this sense, participative decision-making has a strong scale component, although changes in information technologies and associated social patterns may be shifting some aspects of participation towards involvement in electronic communication networks rather than direct personal interactions.

2. We know that many of the systems, processes, and phenomena important to sustainability have characteristic scales. For instance, certain plant and animal species in nature are only viable at certain scales of existence (Thompson, 1942), and certain ecosystems are associated with minimum scales for system maintenance and often maximum scales at which necessary environmental conditions exist, because those conditions vary spatially. Clark (1985) has shown that major systems encompassed by global change processes generally operate at different geographical (and temporal) scales. Since sustainability actions are generally system-specific, the significance of scale is obvious.

3. We know that in many cases existing spatial-administrative frameworks, emerging from other concerns, are not necessarily a good fit with the scales of sustainable development systems and processes (see also Swart and Raes, 2007). Familiar cases include administrative boundaries defined by rivers, where many issues involve drainage basins, and regional patterns of air pollution that cross boundaries between sources and affected areas.

4. Within this complex pattern of often incompatible mosaics, we know that different scales tend to have different potentials and different limitations for action. To oversimplify considerably, local scales offer potentials for participation, flexibility and innovativeness, while larger scales offer potentials for resource mobilization and cost-sharing. The advantages of integrating these kinds of assets across scales would seem to be obvious, but in fact integration is profoundly impeded by differences in who decides, who pays, and who benefits; and perceptions of different scales by other scales often reflect striking ignorance and misunderstanding. As just one example, consider the lack of attention to local agency in many sustainable development initiatives at the international scale, including the Millennium Development Goals and the UNDP adaptation policy framework.

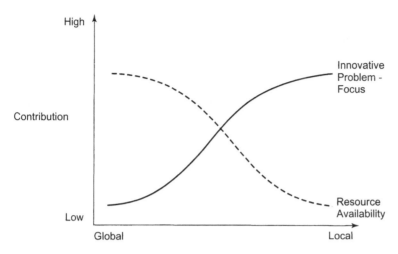

FIGURE 2 Differences between scales in their potentials to support action.

The central challenge is overcoming this current mismatch among scales. The paradox is that resource availability is predominantly top-down, while innovativeness and problem focus are predominantly bottom-up (see Figure 2). In recent years, there have been a number of calls for innovative co-management structures that cross scales in order to promote sustainable development (e.g. Brasseurs and Rosenbaum, 2003; Cash et al., 2006; Sayer and Campbell, 2006).

5. Potentials for integrating actions at different scales

What, then, might be done to realize the potentials for integrating actions at different scales, to make them far more complementary and reinforcing? In many cases, experience to date suggests that initiatives undertaken at relatively large scales – at least in government – often discourage local agency by bogging down relatively localized (sectoral as well as geographical) action in bureaucratic requirements as a condition for access to financial and other resources. Top-down sustainability initiatives are often preoccupied with input accountability, such as criteria for partner selection and justification (often based on relatively detailed quantitative analyses of such attributes as 'additionality'), rather than on outcome metrics such as whether the results make a demonstrable contribution to sustainability (regarding metrics, see NAS, 2005).

Perhaps encouraging and facilitating local agency without bogging everything down calls for a more sophisticated understanding of how scale relationships work. One study, for example, concludes that what local agency needs in order to initiate significant actions for greenhouse gas emission reduction are several conditions: (1) growing evidence of impacts on that locality of climate change; (2) policy interventions that directly or indirectly associate emission reductions with incentives and assistance for local innovation; and (3) technology alternatives appropriate to local conditions (AAG, 2003).

More generally, it appears that key factors include:

1. A kind of mutual trust that is, unfortunately, rare between different scales, at least of governmental decision-making, perhaps reflecting a history of hard experience; avenues for improvement include structures for communication and investments in capacity-building, especially at relatively local scales.

2. Roles of intermediary third parties, facilitating cross-scale interactions through personal relationships and associated structures. There is some evidence that communications through expert-to-expert linkages are more effective than communications through government-to-government linkages (Cash and Moser, 2000), which suggests the importance of local-scale capacity-building where local expertise is limited.
3. Infrastructures for identifying and disseminating information about success experiences, so that individual cases generate benefits beyond their own narrow boundaries.
4. Leadership at any and all scales, which is often the 'hidden' factor in determining whether sustainability barriers are overcome and potentials are realized, including challenges in scale integration.

6. Climate change adaptation as an example

Using climate change as a 'lens' for focusing on key sustainable development issues (Robinson, 2005), a salient example of scale issues for sustainability is climate change adaptation, which is deeply entangled in initiatives that cross scales. The central challenge is that most effective adaptation responses are determined at a local scale: 'one size does not fit all' (SEI, 2004). At the same time, many effective adaptation responses depend on structures and resources at global and national scales (AAG, 2003).

Too often, top-down and bottom-up initiatives work at cross purposes. As suggested above, actions at larger scales can overshadow, discourage and suppress local initiatives by reflecting larger-scale agendas in standardized bureaucratic structures that complicate access to resources. Examples include access by relatively small decision agents to greenhouse gas emission reduction resources through the UNFCCC clean development mechanism (CDM), which requires sophisticated quantitative analyses of 'additionality' and tends to give preference to relatively large incremental savings. At the same time, actions at local scales can undermine larger-scale initiatives through political opposition or downright obstruction, by passive resistance such as a denial of useful information, and/or by local redirections. Where voluntary local initiatives are not sufficient to meet needs for sustainable climate-change-related actions, the challenge is to find ways to combine the strengths of both scales rather than having them work against each other.

Consider, for example, certain strengths offered by both internal and external assets for relatively local-scale climate change adaptation initiatives. Internally, from a local perspective, factors of importance include wealth (or the lack of it); a capacity for collective social action (or the lack of it); economic diversification (or the lack of it); and local leadership (or the lack of it). Externally, factors of importance include linkages that expand the range of alternatives for the locality; financial and human resources, commodities and information; structures that enable adaptive responses such as market and non-market incentives and mechanisms for coordination; risk-sharing approaches such as insurance; and portfolios of locally appropriate technologies.

Perhaps top-down strategies to encourage and support local adaptation should be tailored for differences in local contexts (Figure 3), with localities offering significant current assets treated differently from localities with very limited current assets, and situations where larger-scale structures have a great deal to offer treated differently from structures with very little to offer. For instance, a locality blessed with both substantial external enabling structures and substantial internal assets for action can adapt if it has access to resources. A locality with limited external enabling structures but substantial internal assets needs attention to external linkages and structures, such as access to information about adaptation alternatives. A locality with substantial external enabling structures but limited internal assets needs attention to internal constraints,

		External Factors: Enabling Structures Offering Resources For Adaptation	
		H	L
Internal Factors: Local Agency Offering Current Assets for Adaptation	H	Access to resources	Enhancement of external linkages
	L	Attention to local constraints	Longer term capacity-building

FIGURE 3 Top-down strategies to encourage and support adaptation should consider differences in local contexts.

such as a lack of local leadership. A locality with neither kind of assets is not a promising prospect for adaptation without longer-term capacity-building. In any case, the aim should be to move a locality up and to the left in its capacities for adaptation, where access to resources is the only significant limitation on appropriate adaptive behaviour.

Complicating the development of effective adaptation strategies, however carefully tailored to combinations of large and small-scale contexts, are a variety of issues that are also scale-related. In some, perhaps many, cases there are limits to the potential for adaptation to manage local risks and impacts; examples include changes in natural ecosystems and exposure to extreme weather events (Wilbanks et al., 2007a). A second complication is that priorities for the allocation of top-down resources often need to consider a number of metrics that can point in different directions; for instance emphasizing prospects for payoffs from adaptation investments may favour relatively advantaged localities, while emphasizing equity may favour relatively disadvantaged locations. Moreover, at the current time there are widespread uncertainties about the magnitude and rate of change in risks that adaptation would address, which tends to focus climate change adaptation strategies on actions that also reduce stresses associated with current sustainability challenges and/or risks associated with climate variability, apart from longer-term change (Wilbanks et al., 2007b).

7. Conclusions

Geographical scale is not the only key to sustainability; and its main importance is not theoretical or conceptual, although scale matters in a wide variety of aspects of driving forces, impacts, and responses to sustainable development challenges. Scale matters most because it is directly related to how and where governance decisions are made that affect sustainable development. Most especially, it is salient at this time because different geographical scales of decision-making, from global to local, are not being coordinated and integrated in the interests of sustainability. New approaches to multi-scale action, rooted in a new kind of mutual sensitivity, are needed if sustainable development is to overcome a host of obstacles, both short term and long term.

References

AAG, 2003, *Global Change and Local Places: Estimating, Understanding, and Reducing Greenhouse Gases*, Association of American Geographers, Cambridge University Press, Cambridge, UK.

Brasseurs, H., Rosenbaum, W. (eds), 2003, *Achieving Sustainable Development: The Challenge of Governance Across Scales*, Praeger, New York.

Burch, S., Robinson, J., 2007, 'A framework for explaining the links between capacity and action in response to global climate change', *Climate Policy* 7(4), 304–316.

Burton, I., Bizikova, L., Dickinson, T., Howard, Y., 2007, 'Integrating adaptation into policy: upscaling evidence from local to global', *Climate Policy* 7(4), 371–376.

Capistrano, D., et al., 2003, 'Dealing with scale', in: *Conceptual Framework: Millennium Ecosystem Assessment*, Island Press, Kuala Lumpur, 107–126.

Cash, D., Moser, S., 2000, 'Linking global and local scales: designing dynamic assessment and management processes', *Global Environmental Change* 10, 109–120.

Cash, D.W., Adger, W.N., Berkes, F., Garden, P., Lebel, L., Olsson, P., Pritchard, L., Young, O., 2006, 'Scale and cross-scale dynamics: governance and information in a multilevel world', *Ecology and Society* 11(2), 8–19.

Clark, W., 1985, 'Scales of climate impacts', *Climate Change* 7, 5–27.

Costanza, R., Low, B.S., Ostrom, E., Wilson, J., (eds), 2000, *Institutions, Ecosystems, and Sustainability*, CRC, Baca Raton, FL.

Cutter, S., Richardson, D., Wilbanks, T., 2003, *The Geographical Dimensions of Terrorism*, Routledge, New York.

Eriksen, S., O'Brien, K., 2007, 'Vulnerability, poverty and the need for sustainable adaptation measures', *Climate Policy* 7(4), 337–352.

Hagerstrand, T., 1975, 'Space, time and human conditions', in: A. Karlqvist, L. Lundqvist, F. Snickars (eds), *Dynamic Allocation of Urban Space*, Saxon House, Farnborough, UK, 3–12.

Harvey, D., 1989, *The Growth of Postmodernity*, Johns Hopkins University, Baltimore, MD.

Holling, C., 1995, 'Sustainability: the cross-scale dimension', in: M. Munasinghe, W. Shearer (eds), *Defining and Measuring Sustainability: The Biogeophysical Foundations*, World Bank, Washington, DC, 65–75.

Kates, R., Wilbanks, T., 2003, 'Making the global local: responding to climate change concerns from the bottom up', *Environment* 45(3), 12–23.

Kates, R., et al., 2001, 'Sustainability science', *Science* 292, 641–642.

Meyer, W., Gregory, D., Turner, B., McDowell, P., 1992, 'The local–global continuum', in: R. Abler, M. Marcus, J. Olson (eds), *Geography's Inner Worlds*, Rutgers University, New Brunswick, NJ, 255–279.

Millennium Ecosystem Assessment, 2005, *Ecosystems and Human Well-being. Vol. 4: Multiscale Assessments*, Island Press, Washington, DC.

NAS, 1999, *Our Common Journey: A Transition Toward Sustainability*, National Academy Press, Washington, DC.

NAS, 2005, *Thinking Strategically: The Appropriate Use of Metrics for the Climate Change Science Program*, US National Academies of Science/National Research Council, National Academies Press, Washington, DC.

Parkes, D., Thrift, N., 1980, *Times, Spaces, and Places*, Wiley, New York.

Purvis, M., Grainger, A., 2004, *Exploring Sustainable Development: Geographical Perspectives*, Earthscan, London.

Rebozatti, C., 1993, 'Territory, scale and sustainable development', in: E. Becker, T. Jahn (eds), *Sustainability and the Social Sciences*, Zed Books, London.

Reid, W., Berkes, F., Wilbanks, T., Capistrano, D. (eds), 2006a, *Bridging Scales and Knowledge Systems: Linking Global Science and Local Knowledge in Assessments*, Island Press, Washington, DC.

Reid, W., Berkes, F., Wilbanks, T., Capistrano, D., 2006b. 'Conclusions: bridging scales and knowledge systems,' in: W. Reid, F. Berkes, T. Wilbanks, D. Capistrano (eds), *Bridging Scales and Knowledge Systems: Linking Global Science and Local Knowledge in Assessments*, Island Press, Washington, DC, 296–309.

Robinson, J., 2005, 'Climate change and sustainable development: changing the lens', Paper presented at IPCC Expert Meeting on Adaptation–Mitigation and Sustainable Development, La Reunion, February 2005.

Sayer, J., Campbell, B., 2006, *The Science of Sustainable Development: Local Livelihoods and the Global Environment*, Cambridge University Press, Cambridge, UK.

SEI, 2004, *Enhancing Capacity for Adaptation to Climate Change in Developing Coountries*, Report on Adaptation Research Workshop, New Delhi, November 2003, Stockholm Environment Institute, Oxford, UK.

Swart, R., Raes, F., 2007, 'Making integration of adaptation and mitigation work: mainstreaming into sustainable development policies?', *Climate Policy* 7(4), 288–303.

Thompson, D., 1942, *On Growth and Form*, Cambridge University Press, Cambridge, UK.

Turner, B.L., Kasperson, R.E., Meyer, W.B., Dow, K.M., Golding, D., Kasperson, J.X., Mitchell, R.C., Ratick, S.J., 1990, 'Two types of global environmental change: definitional and spatial-scale issues in their human dimensions', *Global Environmental Change* 1, 14–22.

Wilbanks, T., 1994, '"Sustainable development" in geographic context', *Annals of the Association of American Geographers* 84, 541–557.

Wilbanks, T., 2003a, 'Geographic scaling issues in integrated assessments of climate change', in: J. Rotmans, D. Rothman (eds), *Scaling Issues in Integrated Assessment*, Swets and Zeitlinger, Lisse, The Netherlands, 5–34.

Wilbanks, T., 2003b, 'Geography and technology', in: S. Brunn, S. Cutter, J. Harrington (eds), *Technology and Geography: A Social History*, Kluwer, Dordrecht, The Netherlands, 3–16.

Wilbanks, T., 2003c, 'Integrating climate change and sustainable development in a place-based context', *Climate Policy* 3(S1), S147–S154.

Wilbanks, T., 2005, 'Issues in developing a capacity for integrated analysis of mitigation and adaptation', *Environmental Science and Policy* 8, 541–547.

Wilbanks, T., 2006, 'How scale matters: some concepts and findings', in: W. Reid, F. Berkes, T. Wilbanks, D. Capistrano (eds), *Bridging Scales and Knowledge Systems: Linking Global Science and Local Knowledge in Assessments*, Island Press, Washington, DC, 25–40.

Wilbanks, T., Kates, R., 1999, 'Global change in local places', *Climatic Change* 43(3), 601–628.

Wilbanks, T., Leiby, P., Perlack, R., Ensminger, J.T., Wright, S.B., 2007a, 'Toward an integrated analysis of mitigation and adaptation: some preliminary findings', *Mitigation and Adaptation Strategies for Global Change* 12(5), 713–725.

Wilbanks, T., et al., 2007b, 'Climate change vulnerabilities and responses in a developing country city', *Environment* 49(5), 22–33.

■ synthesis article

Making integration of adaptation and mitigation work: mainstreaming into sustainable development policies?

ROB SWART[1]*, FRANK RAES[2]

[1] Netherlands Environmental Assessment Agency (MNP), PO Box 303, 3720 AH Bilthoven, The Netherlands
[2] Joint Research Centre of the European Union, Institute for Environment and Sustainability (JRC-IES), Via E. Fermi 1,
I 21020 Ispra, Italy

Can an integrated approach to mitigation and adaptation offer opportunities for a more effective response to climate change than the current strategies? The nature of the linkages depends on the dimensions: economic, institutional or environmental, and on the scale. Differences are pervasive: adaptation and mitigation usually have different temporal and spatial scales and are mostly relevant for different economic sectors, so that costs and benefits are distributed differently. The article concludes that generally the global, regional and – in most countries – national potential of synergetic options to mitigate and adapt to climate change is relatively low, and both strategies should be considered as complementary. However, a few notable exceptions are identified in the land and water management and urban planning sectors, in particular in countries or locations where these sectors provide important adaptation and mitigation opportunities. What is the theoretically most efficient and least expensive mixture of adaptation and mitigation policies may not be a very urgent policy question. Instead, five pragmatic ways of broadening climate policy are suggested, while taking into account the linkages between adaptation and mitigation: (1) *avoiding trade-offs* – when designing policies for mitigation or adaptation, (2) *identifying synergies*, (3) *enhancing response capacity*, (4) *developing institutional links* between adaptation and mitigation – e.g. in national institutions and in international negotiations, and (5) *mainstreaming* adaptation and mitigation considerations into broader sustainable development policies.

Keywords: adaptive capacity; climate change; mitigative capacity; policy formation; sustainable development; synergy

Une approche intégrant mitigation et adaptation peut-elle donner lieu à des opportunités de lutte contre le changement climatique plus efficaces que les stratégies actuelles? La nature des liens dépend des dimensions économiques, institutionnelles ou environnementales et de l'échelle. Les différences sont omniprésentes : adaptation et mitigation ont habituellement lieu à différentes échelles de temps et d'espace afin de distribuer les coûts et bénéfices de manière différente. L'article conclut qu'en général, le potentiel mondial, régional et, pour la plupart des pays, national, des options agissant en synergie pour la mitigation et l'adaptation au changement climatique est relativement faible, et que les deux stratégies devraient être considérées en complément l'une de l'autre. Cependant, quelques exceptions notables sont identifiées dans les secteurs de la gestion urbaine, du sol et de l'eau, surtout dans les pays ou régions où ces secteurs offrent des possibilités importante pour les actions d'adaptation et de mitigation. Ce que serait en principe le mélange de politiques d'adaptation et de mitigation le plus efficace et le moins coûteux, n'est pas en soi une question politique de grande urgence. Nous suggérons de préférence cinq manières concrètes d'élargir la politique climatique, tout en prenant compte des liens entre adaptation et mitigation: (a) éviter les compromis – lors de l'élaboration de politiques de mitigation et d'adaptation (b) discerner les synergies (c) augmenter la capacité de réaction (d) développer les liens institutionnels entre adaptation et mitigation – par exemple dans les instances nationales et les négociations internationales (e) incorporer adaptation et mitigation dans les politiques de développement durable plus larges.

Mots clés: capacités adaptives; capacités de mitigation; changement climatique; développement durable; élaboration de politiques; synergie

■ *Corresponding author. E-mail*: Rob.Swart@rivm.nl

© 2007 Earthscan ISSN: 1469-3062 (print), 1752-7457 (online) www.climatepolicy.com

1. Background and objectives

Both mitigation of and adaptation to climate change have the same purpose: reducing its undesirable consequences. However, for historical reasons, the two have been separated both in science and in policy.[1] The definition of the two concepts by the Intergovernmental Panel on Climate Change (IPCC) reinforces the separation: mitigation has been defined as 'anthropogenic intervention to reduce the sources or enhance the sinks of greenhouse gases' and adaptation as 'adjustment in natural or human systems in response to actual or expected climatic stimuli or their effects, which moderates harm or exploits beneficial opportunities' (IPCC, 2001). The distinction is also reflected by the Working Group structure of the IPCC. One of the reasons that adaptation was not only treated separately but also received little attention at the beginning of the climate change negotiations was that – especially in Europe – an emphasis on adaptation was suggested in order to take away the urgency of mitigation. In the early 1990s, climate change was still considered to be merely an environmental problem that could be addressed in a fashion similar to that of acid rain and stratospheric ozone depletion, with a targets and timetable approach aiming at mitigating the impacts (Munasinghe and Swart, 2004). Also the perceived larger uncertainties involved in adaptation (where, by whom, to what?) played a role in lower levels of attention to adaptation. Finally, while the signs of climate change increased, until recently no significant changes in human or ecological systems could be definitely attributed to climate change. With some exceptions, discussed below, in the United Nations Framework Convention on Climate Change, mitigation and adaptation are generally separated. Although the ultimate objective of the UNFCCC (Article 2) on avoiding dangerous interference with the climate system implicitly involves adaptation, the emphasis on stabilization of greenhouse gas concentrations in the atmosphere also tends to focus the attention on long-term mitigation rather than reducing vulnerability to climate change or adapting to it in the shorter term. According to Pielke (2004), the UNFCCC definition of climate change leads to a bias against adaptation, since adaptation – according to the UNFCCC definition – should be limited to changes that are proven to be anthropogenic. The broader definition of climate change of the IPCC includes natural as well as anthropogenic causes and hence does not have the same bias against adaptation.

Until recently, mitigation was considered to be a problem of developed countries, which had caused the problem and not only had the responsibility but also the resources to do something about it. Adaptation was more a problem of developing countries, where per capita emissions were low and vulnerability high. Gradually, it has become clear that climate change, with its roots in the fundamental requirements of societies for energy and food, may rather be framed as a development issue rather than as an environmental problem. But even if developing countries may be more vulnerable, climate change also affects developed countries. Throughout the world many developments in society are increasing exposure and sensitivity to current climate variability, regardless of the level of climate change, such as habitation of marginal and low-lying lands, increased water and food demands, and dependence on highly technical interdependent systems. This makes adaptation increasingly relevant (Pielke, 1998).

Only in the last decade has policy attention to adaptation started to increase, because of the attribution of observed impacts to climate change and the increased recognition of vulnerability developing countries in particular. It is also significant that, following a rapid start in 1992 with an international framework convention (without binding obligations), when it came to formal commitments, international negotiations about climate change mitigation made progress only very slowly. Mitigation and adaptation both aim at reducing risks of negative climate change impacts, and are obviously closely linked in different ways. Risks from climate change can be expressed by the simple equations:

$$risk = probability * climate\ hazard * vulnerability$$

and

$$vulnerability = exposure * sensitivity/adaptive\ capacity[2]$$

Mitigation aims at reducing the climate change effect, adaptation aims at reducing vulnerability to these effects. The latter can be achieved by reducing the exposure to climate change, by reducing the sensitivity, or by enhancing the capacity to adapt. According to these formulas, eventually more mitigation requires less adaptation and vice versa. This raises the question of whether an integrated approach could offer benefits over two independent, parallel strategies and, if so, how. This question is central to this article.

The literature on integrated approaches is rather sparse. In its Third Assessment Report, the IPCC included a preliminary assessment of the linkages between adaptation and mitigation (Toth et al., 2001). Toth et al. (2001) argue that the global political commitment to stabilize greenhouse gas concentrations and the physical commitment of the climate system to change because of past, current and unavoidable future greenhouse gas emissions implies that there is no choice between either mitigating or adapting, but that both have to be pursued. The question, however, is what the best share and timing of both would be, and how they can best be implemented.

This early IPCC assessment of the links between adaptation and mitigation was still rather abstract. The objective of this article is to explore in more concrete terms what the links are, and how they may be used to further climate policy development, capturing synergies between adaptation and mitigation, and avoiding trade-offs. To understand the nature of the two approaches, in the next section we first summarize the differences and then identify the links between them. In Section 3, we discuss the importance of different dimensions and scales. We then turn to more concrete examples of synergies and trade-offs in Section 4. In Section 5 we place the two options in the broader context of sustainable development, and in Section 6 we summarize our main findings and formulate five recommendations for action.

2. Differences and similarities between adaptation and mitigation

At an aggregate level, adaptation affects the costs and benefits of public mitigation policy (Kane and Shogren, 2000). At least theoretically, an optimum balance between adaptation and mitigation would be possible, and hence integrated analysis may provide useful insights. From this same economic perspective, limited to climate change response expenditures, increased spending on mitigation would be at the expense of adaptation (e.g. Michaelowa, 2001). There are indeed intrinsic differences between the two types of climate response, leading Dang et al. (2003) to conclude that 'mitigation and adaptation are currently perceived to be mutually exclusive at worst, or parallel strategies at best'. All these views ignore the fact that increases in both mitigation and adaptation efforts may make perfect sense for a society and even the economy in order to decrease climate risks and capture co-benefits. Therefore, before exploring the potential benefits of integrating adaptive and mitigative responses to climate change, it is useful to not only consider their differences, as several other authors have done (e.g. Toth et al., 2001; Tol, 2005), but also their similarities.

Table 1 summarizes the definitions of the types of responses, and the 'common wisdom' as to the different dominant focus of the two approaches. Table 1 also shows some exceptions to this 'common wisdom', and lists some similarities. Pertinent perceived differences are that spatial and temporal scales would be very different. Mitigation would be mainly aimed at addressing a global problem, while adaptation would be aimed at resolving local problems. While this is generally true, concrete mitigative as well as adaptive actions necessarily involve decisions by individuals at the local level. It

TABLE 1 Definitions, differences and similarities between mitigation and adaptation

	Issue	Mitigation		Adaptation	
		Dominant focus	Examples of exceptions	Dominant focus	Examples of exceptions
Definition		Anthropogenic intervention to reduce the sources or enhance the sinks of greenhouse gases		Adjustment in natural or human systems in response to actual or expected climatic stimuli or their effects, which moderates harm or exploits beneficial opportunities	
Differences	Causes/effect	Primarily addresses *causes*	Urban design with low energy requirements and low vulnerability	Primarily addresses *consequences*	Drought-resistant biofuels can address both vulnerability and emissions
	Spatial scale	Main objective avoiding *global* changes	Co-benefits for short-term local air pollution, energy security, jobs	Main objective *local* damage avoidance	Adaptation of temperate farmers may have global consequences
	Sectors	Mainly energy, transport, building and industry sectors	Mitigation options also available in water and land management	Mainly urban planning, water, agriculture, health, coastal zones sectors	Renewable energy sources can be vulnerable
	Time scale	*Long-term* benefit from avoided climate change	Co-benefits for short-term, local air pollution, energy security, jobs	Often main driver *short-term* benefit due to reducing vulnerability to current climate	Preparing for long-term impacts
	Beneficiaries	Mainly benefits *others* (altruistic)	Co-benefits for mitigating actors, local air pollution, energy security, jobs	Mainly benefits *those who implement it* (egoistic)	Some adaptation may have wider benefits
	Incentives	Usually *incentives needed*	No-regrets options (e.g., energy efficiency)	Often *incentives not needed*	Anticipatory actions without immediate benefits may need incentives
	Urgency	*Lower political urgency/* legitimacy	Short-term co-benefits, local air pollution, energy security, jobs enhance urgency	*Higher political urgency/* legitimacy	Proactive adaptation with high costs and uncertain effect can have low urgency
Similarities	Goal	Aiming at reduction of climate change risks			
	Benefits	Having ancillary benefits that may be as important as the climate-related benefits			
	Drivers	Driven by availability/penetration of new technology & societal ability to change			

can also be seen that some adaptation actions can have global consequences; for example, temperate-zone farmers are increasingly competing with tropical farmers by adapting to a warmer climate (T. Downing, 2006, personal communication), drought-resilient cultivars and improved climate predictions can have benefits far beyond the local level. From an economic perspective, the benefits from mitigation are greater at the global scale and external to a local area, while adaptation leads to greater local benefits. Hence, comparisons of mitigation and adaptation generally favour mitigation at a global scale and favour adaptation if performed at a local scale (Wilbanks et al., 2003). Thus, the dominant spatial scales of mitigation and adaptation actions are generally different, but at all geographical levels, mitigation and adaptation both play a role. In the next section we discuss some aspects of the linkages between the two responses at different levels of scale in more detail.

Thus, mitigation eventually aims at stabilizing greenhouse gas concentrations in the atmosphere, something that can only be achieved at long time scales. Adaptive actions often aim at reducing vulnerability not only to future climate change, but also to current climate variability. Again, while this is true in general, it can also be observed that many mitigative actions can also have short-term benefits, e.g. in the form of reduced air pollution,[3] or in some 'no-regrets' cases, in the form of economic benefits. Similarly, proactive adaptive actions may not have any benefit at all at any time scale, if climate changes do not materialize, or if the changes are very different from what is expected. This is mostly relevant for adaptation in the urban sector, where dealing with higher temperatures and higher precipitation can entail significant costs (T. Downing, 2006, personal communication). For adaptation in the management of land, water and resources, the risk of unnecessary adaptation is smaller, since here reduced vulnerability to current climate variability often requires smaller investments and usually does have some benefits regardless of climate change.

Another key difference is that the actors involved in adaptation and mitigation are often different. The main source of greenhouse gases is the combustion of fossil fuels, which involves mainly economic sectors such as energy, transport, industry, and the domestic sectors. With some exceptions (e.g. renewable energy sources such as biofuels, hydropower, wind energy, and solar energy are dependent on climate variables such as precipitation, wind speed and direction, and cloud cover, respectively; cooling water availability of fossil-fuel and nuclear energy), these sectors are generally less vulnerable to the impacts of climatic changes. The economic sectors most vulnerable to climate change are the agricultural, water, and coastal zone management sectors – and these are the sectors that at the global level play a lesser role in emitting greenhouse gases and hence in mitigation. However, primarily economic activities with a spatial, land component can also be relevant for mitigation, such as agriculture, forestry and urban design. In areas where hydropower or availability of cooling water plays an important role in energy supply, and also in the water sector, integration between mitigation and adaptation can be important. These issues are further discussed in Section 4.

Another set of differences has to do with responsibilities. While all may have a moral obligation to contribute to global mitigation of climate change, the direct benefits of mitigative activities usually fall on others, in other places and/or at other times. Mitigation is altruistic and can induce free-riding; incentives to join the global effort are usually required. In contrast, those implementing adaptive actions usually have a direct interest in the effects in terms of reduced vulnerability. Adaptation is egoistic and incentives may be less important. These characteristics of mitigation and adaptation have an effect on the political legitimacy and urgency of action. In both cases, however, the co-benefits may outweigh the climate benefits, but this is often not yet recognized because of the lack of a fully comprehensive evaluation of costs and benefits over time and over different scales. As to the urgency, the perception that mitigation would not be very urgent has recently changed because of increased recognition that global emissions have to peak within the next few decades in order to limit climate change to acceptable levels.

Notwithstanding these pervasive differences, mitigation and adaptation also have some aspects in common. Tompkins and Adger (2005) argue that both depend on the capability of a society to develop and diffuse new technologies and to change its behaviour, and even suggest integrating a society's adaptive and mitigative capacities into a single concept of 'response capacity', an idea also supported by Bizikova et al. (2006). However, while the determinants of adaptive and mitigative capacity are overlapping and mutually supportive, they differ in application. The same capacity may be used to respond to the impacts of climate change or to reduce greenhouse gas emissions (Winkler et al., 2007). This is further elaborated in Section 5.

As noted above, the two strategies have their main goal in common: reducing the risks associated with climate change. Jones (2006) observes that mitigation could be viewed as mainly aiming at reducing the risks of high levels of climate change in the longer term. Its benefits in terms of reduced risks are a function of the level of mitigation and the climate sensitivity. Adaptation can then be viewed as aiming at reducing the risks that remain after reducing the risks of high levels of climate change. Its benefits in terms of reduced damages occur earlier, because current climate risks are also reduced (Jones, 2006). Figure 1 not only suggests that at least theoretically an optimal mix between mitigation, adaptation and residual damage may be found (see below for a discussion on the feasibility), but it also suggests that adaptation and mitigation address two different types of climate risks. Mitigation aims primarily at reducing the risks associated with high levels of climate change and unacceptably high adaptation costs (see Jones, 2006), at mitigation costs, which are still relatively low. However, at some point mitigation costs become increasingly high. Here, adaptation further reduces residual impacts at costs much lower than those associated with unmitigated climate change, and at the same time reduces vulnerability to current climatic changes.

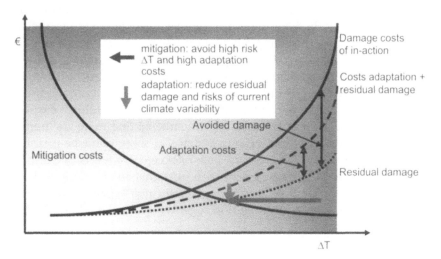

FIGURE 1 Costs of mitigation, adaptation and residual damage of climate change. Total costs of adaptation and residual damage depend on the ratio between adaptation costs and avoided damage. In the Figure it is assumed that the adaptation costs are smaller than the avoided damage. This conceptual Figure is only meaningful at the global level. The shading gets brighter from top to bottom and from right to left, indicating that the brightest, most positive situation would be the lower left corner where both mitigation and impacts/adaptation costs would be lowest; however, unfortunately there are no realistic solutions in this corner.

3. Levels of scale and dimensions of sustainable development

In its Third Assessment Report, the IPCC addressed the search for the best possible combination of adaptation and mitigation strategies, and stressed the importance of different dimensions (Toth et al., 2001). Toth et al. (2001) distinguished between economic, precautionary and institutional considerations, similar to the economic, environmental and social dimensions of sustainable development. At the same time, different processes relevant for mitigation, adaptation and sustainable development have characteristic scales; different scales tend to have different potentials and limitations for action, and existing spatial-administrative frameworks are not necessarily a good fit with the relevant scales (Wilbanks, 2007). In the matrix of Table 2 we have therefore included some examples of approaches that link adaptation and mitigation at different scales and for different dimensions, which we discuss briefly below.

3.1. Global level

In the climate change response literature, the top-left corner of the matrix on global *economic* analysis is most frequently addressed. Integrated assessment models are available that can analyse marginal costs of mitigation and marginal costs of adaptation and residual impacts (Toth et al., 2001). Although theoretically appealing, the scarcity of research results for costs and benefits of adaptation at the global level, the large uncertainties regarding costs and benefits of (avoided) impacts and mitigation, and the problem of damages that can or maybe should not be monetized make a meaningful cost–benefit analysis aiming at determining a most efficient mix of mitigation, adaptation and residual damage extremely difficult. Figure 1 should be regarded as a thought experiment to enhance the understanding of the linkages and differences between adaptation and mitigation, rather than as a basis for a quantified cost–benefit analysis. In practice, at most a comparison of mitigation costs with damage costs, with at most some exogenous simple assumptions for adaptation has been explored by a few authors (Toth et al., 2001; Tol, 2006). Also, even if an economic optimal solution could be identified, this approach generally ignores social, institutional and environmental dimensions (equity, implementation issues, natural ecosystem adaptation, e.g. see Klein et al., 2005). A very recent bold attempt at a global cost–benefit analysis that attracted much media attention was made by Stern (2006), with very rough estimates of damage costs and with conclusions which were heavily influenced by the discount rate assumptions. The IPCC, however, in its Fourth Assessment Report (IPCC, 2007), refrained from doing a cost–benefit analysis for the reasons discussed above. Finally, it should be remembered that there are limits to adaptation and mitigation. Not only will natural and human systems at some point be unable to adapt, but also adaptation or mitigation costs can exceed feasible or acceptable levels (see also Figure 1).

From an *institutional* perspective, it is interesting to note that in the UNFCCC, mitigation and adaptation are both addressed, but that they are generally not explicitly linked. The UNFCCC has several references to adaptation and mitigation together, but generally as parallel approaches. For example, it requires Parties to

> formulate, implement, publish and regularly update national and, where appropriate, regional programmes containing measures to mitigate climate change by addressing anthropogenic emissions by sources and removals by sinks of all greenhouse gases not controlled by the Montreal Protocol, and measures to facilitate adequate adaptation to climate change (UNFCCC, 1992).

It also requires developed country Parties to assist the developing country Parties that are particularly vulnerable to the adverse effects of climate change in meeting the costs of adaptation to those

TABLE 2 Examples of adaptation–mitigation linkages for different scales and three dimensions of sustainable development

	Global	Regional/national	Local
Economic/development dimension	Analyse theoretically optimal shares through cost–benefit analysis	Mainstream climate into development/sector policies, identify most efficient way	Avoid economic trade-offs, research most efficient solution talking into account co-benefits
Examples	*Analyse theoretically optimal shares of mitigation and adaptation action to support international negotiations*	*Include climate change mitigation and adaptation concerns in energy and water policy, spatial planning, development aid*	*Evaluate mitigation potential of renewable energy taking into account possibly increased vulnerability to climate change*
Institutional/social dimension	Negotiate balance adaptation and mitigation actions in UNFCCC context	Link local with global through national/regional SD policies (link different actors)	Enhance adaptive and mitigative capacity, involve stakeholders
Examples	*Account for justice, compensation, common but differentiated responsibility*	*Translate commitments from international agreements into framework for local actors (e.g. EU emissions trading system)*	*Inform local stakeholders (farmers, companies, citizens) about climate change risks and mitigation opportunities*
Environmental/ precautionary dimension	Determine acceptable level of climate change, limits to adaptation (Article 2)	Determine environmentally most effective national policies	Protect ecosystems, health, search synergies
Examples	*Evaluate the EU's 2°C climate goal, taking into account adaptation as well as critical vulnerable ecosystems of global importance*	*Develop ecosystem, water basin management strategies taking into account adaptation and mitigation concerns*	*Manage protected areas taking into account climate change impacts, carbon sink function, and biodiversity*

adverse effects. As a follow-up to the latter point, the Kyoto Protocol stipulates that a share of the proceeds from CDM activities is to be used to assist these vulnerable developing country Parties to meet the costs of adaptation. Another example of a link between mitigation and adaptation in the UNFCCC is the discussion on reducing the impacts of mitigation on countries whose economies are highly dependent on fossil fuels (Article 4.8). This is also part of the UNFCCC's 5-year plan for adaptation (UNFCCC, 2006). However, so far there is no direct link, e.g. countries helping other countries with adaptation actions do not get any (mitigation) credits for this, and countries that do not make any effort to mitigate GHG emissions do not yet have to pay higher side payments to vulnerable countries. In recent UNFCCC discussions on adaptation, some developed countries have suggested closer links between adaptation and mitigation but, so far, key developing countries have stressed the need not to make the issues too complicated, and mitigation remains absent from the UNFCCC's recently agreed 5-year work programme and the methodological toolkit for development and evaluation of adaptation options.

From an *environmental* perspective, the link between adaptation and mitigation at the global level is formalized in the UNFCCC's ultimate objective (Article 2) stipulating the requirement to stabilize concentrations of greenhouse gases and referring to natural adaptation of ecosystems, food security and sustainable economic development. Such links have only just begun to be explored by the scientific community. Adaptation alters the definition of tolerable change and hence would affect mitigation requirements, e.g. as analysed in the German guardrail or tolerable windows approach, which tries to operationalize the UNFCCC objective (Yohe and Toth, 2000). From a strong sustainability perspective and a strict interpretation of the precautionary principle, the most vulnerable area (high exposure, low adaptive capacity) would set the standard for global mitigation. From a weak sustainability perspective, trade-offs with social and economic dimensions have to be taken to account and a certain level of environmental impacts may have to be tolerated if this leads to less damage on the social and/or economic scores. This provides negotiation space for determining what constitutes dangerous interference with the climate system, dependent on the risk attitudes of the negotiators.

3.2. Regional and national level

Moving from the global to the regional, national and local scales, the costs and benefits of adaptation, mitigation and impacts will change, and hence the cost–benefit ratio of response options is very dependent on the scale. Equally, capturing adaptation and mitigation in one model makes little sense, because methods and tools for adaptation and for mitigation typically have different spatial and temporal scales, and relevant actors and sectors are often different and disconnected. We agree with Tol (2005) that adaptation and mitigation cannot be meaningfully compared, especially at lower levels. For example, mitigation action would still be justified if the costs of mitigation in a developed country were to be higher than the costs of inaction for that same country, because of the benefits in other regions.

At the national and regional level (e.g. the EU), governmental institutions can play a role by encouraging the integration of both mitigation and adaptation considerations into sectoral policies, not as competitors for scarce resources but as potentially equally important elements of comprehensive policy development in a broader context of sustainable development. These institutions have an intermediary role to play in ensuring proper linkages between global risks and responsibilities, and the mainly local implementation of mitigation and adaptation actions, and in providing a proper framework to arrive at the most effective solutions. In addition, national institutions play a key role in enhancing mitigative and adaptive capacity through their determinants. This is discussed further in Section 5. From the environmental perspective, national governments should ensure the environmental integrity of climate change response policies. For example, governments should ensure that biofuels are produced sustainably, or that coastal protection infrastructure does not affect ecologically valuable areas.

3.3. Local level

Many adaptation and mitigation actions are implemented at the local level. Particularly at this level, knowledge about climate change is often limited and climate change is generally one of the less urgent considerations in planning processes. Linking the global long-term problem of climate change with local priorities is a challenge (Wilbanks, 2005). Participatory approaches can play a key role here (e.g. Bizikova et al., 2006). For specific climate response actions, rather than searching for optimal combinations of adaptation and mitigation, it appears to make more sense to routinely include mitigation consequences in a comprehensive (cost–benefit) analysis of adaptation projects and to include vulnerability and adaptation consequences as one of many aspects of mitigation actions. Developing local plans and projects, economic as well as environmental aspects of mitigation and adaptation should be considered. Institutionally, at the local level, joint efforts between local governments, citizens and the private sector can enhance adaptive and mitigative capacity. In the next section, we focus more on synergies and trade-offs of concrete actions.

4. Synergies and trade-offs

In general – with some notable exceptions discussed below – most mitigation options have little direct consequence for vulnerability to climate change. We also consider indirect effects, such as increased vulnerability of populations because of mitigation expenditures, as generally being very small.[4] Similarly, most adaptation options have relatively few consequences for global climate change – even if adaptation projects may increase energy use and associated GHG emissions at the local scale. In most economic sectors, the number of concrete options that both reduce vulnerability to climate change and reduce GHG emissions (or enhance sinks) is relatively small. However, at a more detailed level, for specific sectors and locations, there are important exceptions. Table 3 summarizes some examples of synergetic options and trade-offs.[5] It comes as no surprise that most entries in Table 3 are in sectors which are important for both adaptation and mitigation; notably land (land use, urban planning, housing, agriculture and forestry) and water (water supply, hydropower, cooling water).

4.1. Synergies

Two types of synergies can be distinguished. Indirectly, mitigation can lead to reduced stresses other than climate change, reducing vulnerability to climate change. For example, reduced air pollution as a side effect of climate policies can lead to lower health impacts and consequently higher resistance to climate stresses. The same applies to ecosystem vitality. Synergetic options that more directly combine reduced greenhouse gas emissions and reduced vulnerability can mainly be found in three areas: urban and infrastructure planning, water resource management, and land-use and forestry.

Climate change adaptation and mitigation can come together in the planning of urban areas, notably in locations that are vulnerable to climate change. Urban design could pay proper attention to climate-safe siting, energy-conserving building characteristics (adapted building codes), and low transportation requirements. This would both limit energy use (and associated GHG emissions) and also reduce exposure to the possible negative consequences of climate change, e.g. in low-lying coastal areas or areas prone to flooding. At the urban level, climate change has just recently become an issue that is taken into account. Examples are initiatives in Finland (Peltonen et al., 2005), the CitiesPlus programme in Canada, which combines mitigation, adaptation and enhanced resilience (Sheltair, 2003), and METREX, a network of European metropolitan areas that has started to explore ways to respond to climate change.

Also in the land-use and forestry sectors synergies can be found. Reforestation to prevent flooding and erosion sequesters carbon. However, the types of trees best suited to preventing flooding and protecting biodiversity may not be the most effective from a carbon sequestration point of view (e.g. Dang et al., 2003). IPCC (2007) identifies synergetic options primarily for the rural poor in the least developed countries, where soil conservation (storing carbon), low water requirements, and biofuel production (reducing emissions) can go hand in hand. Also, forestry mitigation projects (e.g. forest conservation, afforestation and reforestation, biomass energy plantations, agro-forestry, urban forestry) can lower water evaporation and lower vulnerability to heat stress (IPCC, 2007).

In the water sector, the development of hydropower facilities can reduce fossil-fuel-related energy use and reduce dependency on foreign energy imports. If properly designed, the associated water storage can also limit vulnerability to precipitation variability and to climate change. However, there can also be trade-offs (see below).

The link between CDM mitigation activities and the climate adaptation fund has already been mentioned above. Using an example from Vietnam, Dang et al. (2003) suggest putting the search for synergies into practice by actively identifying opportunities for CDM projects which decrease vulnerability to climate change next to reducing GHG emissions, increasing the host country's ability to deal with climate risks, and facilitating a more active role of developing countries in the UNFCCC and Kyoto Protocol process.

TABLE 3 Examples of synergies and trade-offs between direct adaptive and mitigative responses to climate change (see also Bizikova et al., 2006). Changing social or institutional capabilities and changing development paths are not included since these are indirectly influencing greenhouse gas emissions, sinks, exposure and sensitivity

Mitigation → Adaptation ↓	Actions decreasing GHG emissions, enhancing sinks, protecting carbon stocks	Actions enhancing GHG emissions, reducing sinks, destroying carbon stocks
Actions decreasing exposure and sensitivity (vulnerability) to climate change	*Synergies (also contributing to wider sustainable development goals)* Increase energy efficiency/reduce energy dependency Increase water use efficiency/reduce water consumption Protect soils, plant trees, develop agro-forestry (carbon storage) Improve forest fire management (early warning, fire fighting) Produce crops matching local climate and local needs Improve health through clean energy with less pollution Enhance ecosystem resilience by reduced air pollution Design urban areas with high level of protection, high density and low energy use Expand parks and other green spaces in/around cities Design appropriate building codes/standards (climate-resistant and energy-efficient, e.g. natural ventilation or renewable energy for cooling)	*Trade-offs of adaptation ('adaptive emissions')* Use fossil-based electricity for air conditioning, cooling of buildings and water supply (e.g., desalinization), Strengthen coastal protection infrastructure (energy use) Expand fossil-fuel-energized irrigation of lands, Adapt temperate farmers competing with tropical farmers Expand crop area/number of annual crops to capture benefits of warming in relevant areas Include mitigation in development aid, research programmes at the expense of adaptation
Actions increasing exposure and sensitivity (vulnerability) to climate change	*Trade-offs of mitigation ('new vulnerabilities')* Building low-emissions facilities (e.g. renewable/nuclear power plants) in vulnerable areas) Implement mitigation policies with costs that affect income of the vulnerable poor Increasing dependence on too narrow climate-sensitive renewable energy Establish large-scale biofuel production driving locals to vulnerable areas Include adaptation in development aid, research programmes at the expense of mitigation	*Actions contributing to unsustainable development* Destroy forests, emitting carbon and increasing vulnerability to drought Develop urban areas in low-lying areas with little natural cooling or long travel distances, and high vulnerability to flooding

4.2. Trade-offs

The most obvious example of trade-offs of adaptation actions for mitigation is the fact that many adaptation options, such as coastal protection infrastructure, additional cooling requirements and expanded irrigation, all increase energy use, often with associated GHG emissions, and thus increase the need for mitigation ('adaptive emissions'; Bizikova et al., 2006).

An interesting example of trade-offs of adaptation options for mitigation is in the winter sports sector. To make up for the decreasing snowfall, artificial snowmaking is rapidly increasing its importance, even pushing the industry into areas that were formerly less suitable for skiing. In Austria, 40% of the ski areas are currently equipped with artificial snow facilities, and an expansion to 90% is foreseen, with large water and energy requirements (K. Radunski, 2006, personal communication). This development in one key economic sector surely does not help Austria in meeting its Kyoto target and one may wonder how sustainable this practice will be with continuing warming trends.

Trade-offs of mitigation activities for adaptation are less obvious ('new vulnerabilities'; see Bizikova et al., 2006). A higher dependency on hydropower can also increase the vulnerability to decreased precipitation because of climate change in some regions. Also, large dams can lead to methane emissions which can offset part of the GHG gains (e.g. World Commission on Dams, 2000). The magnitude and time period are, however, still fiercely debated (e.g. Fearnside, 2006; Rosa et al., 2006). Theoretically global mitigation could alter the relative valuation of different development projects such as hydropower plants because of missing benefits (Yohe et al., 2007), just as mitigation may lower the profitability of agriculture in areas that are projected to benefit from climate change. Another example of a potential trade-off is the shift of people to more vulnerable areas as a result of large-scale biofuel plantations.

5. Enhancing response capacity and mainstreaming

The IPCC Third Assessment Report (TAR) introduced the term mitigative capacity as a mirror image of adaptive capacity, a term that had already been in use for some time in impacts and vulnerability analysis. The TAR defined mitigative capacity as 'the ability to diminish the intensity of the natural and other stresses to which it might be exposed' (Banuri and Weyant, 2001), where adaptive capacity relates to the reduction of exposure or sensitivity to these stresses. Winkler et al. (2007) note that this definition suggests that only large countries or groups have a mitigative capacity in the sense of influencing global climate change, and suggest as an alternative definition 'the ability to reduce greenhouse gas emissions or enhance natural sinks'. The TAR suggests the following determinants of mitigative capacity:

- a range of viable technological options for reducing emissions
- a range of viable policy instruments with which the country might effect the adoption of these options
- a structure of critical institutions and the derivative allocation of decision-making authority
- the availability and distribution of resources required to underwrite their adoption and the associated, broadly defined opportunity costs of devoting those resources to mitigation
- a stock of human capital, including education and personal security
- a stock of social capital, including the definition of property rights
- a country's access to risk-spreading processes (e.g. insurance, options and futures markets, etc.)
- the ability of decision-makers to manage information, the processes by which these decision-makers determine which information is credible, and the credibility of the decision-makers themselves.

If we replace 'emissions' in the first item by 'vulnerability and exposure', we can see that the determinants of adaptive capacity are basically the same. Hence, as noted in the Introduction, enhancing these determinants would increase both adaptive and mitigative capacity, which brings some authors to suggest combining the two into one concept of response capacity (Tompkins and Adger, 2005; Bizikova et al., 2006).

However, it is important to note that actual capacities may be unevenly distributed between the relevant actors. Capacities have to be built both in institutions that address mitigation and in those that have to deal with adaptation, which can be very different. While the two types of capacities are very similar and are rooted in the same development basis, they can differ strongly in application (Winkler et al., 2007). When the response capacity has to be translated into action, the differences between the two types of response re-emerge. If the capacity is used to adapt, the benefit may be direct and local, and if it is used to mitigate, it would be indirect and global (if co-benefits are not taken into account). It is usually not possible or relevant for individuals, groups or companies to both adapt and mitigate at the same time. While, for farmers, water managers or coastal inhabitants, climate change adaptation may be relevant or even urgent, for most of the other citizens in both developing and industrialized countries it is not a matter of priority. For the poor in developing countries, mitigation is not very urgent or even very relevant.

In general, one may say that in most industrialized countries all or almost all the criteria for an effective adaptive and mitigative capacity are satisfied, and political determination, individual priorities and sustained efforts are likely to be important factors determining the actual level of adaptation and mitigation. However, for reasons of political economy, countries might not apply their capacity to respond (Michaelowa, 2001). In industrialized countries, the emphasis needs to be on applying the existing capacity. However, in most developing countries there is ample scope for improving on these determinants, which would be a necessary requirement for action. However, as in industrialized countries, the capacity alone would also be insufficient to actually adapt and/or mitigate and similar difficulties will arise when putting capacity into action.

Just as the adaptive and mitigative capacities are determined by the level and type of development, so the greenhouse gas emissions and the vulnerability to climate change are usually determined by the level and type of development at least as much as by specific adaptation or mitigation policies. Therefore, for an effective climate change response, it is urgent to include climate change considerations into the development of more generic development policies. At COP-8, the UNFCCC recommended integrating climate change objectives into other policy areas (UNFCCC, 2002). While to some extent this is being pursued in particular areas, such as in multilateral development collaboration (e.g. Burton and van Aalst, 2004; Agrawala, 2005) and at the local, urban level (e.g. the Cities for Climate Protection (CCP) campaign – see http://www.iclei.org/), it is in general not yet a common feature of national and sectoral policy-making. Also, mainstreaming climate change considerations into broader development policies appears to be more often suggested for developing countries (e.g. Huq et al., 2003) than for developed countries, at least until very recently. The broad, long-term strategy on sustainable development of the European Commission (EC, 2001) suggested addressing the priority problem of climate change only through a number of specific climate and energy policies rather than suggesting, in addition, integrating climate change considerations into the much broader set of European policies. The subsequent action plan *Winning the Battle against Global Climate Change* (EC, 2005) does mention links with other policy areas merely in the context of broadening the scope of the international negotiations rather than mainstreaming in Europe itself. However, in the recent communication of the European Commission on *Limiting Global Climate Change to 2 Degrees Celsius: The Way Ahead for 2020 and Beyond* (EC, 2007a) and its Green Paper on Adaptation (EC, 2007b), mainstreaming of mitigation and adaptation in other European policies is now proposed more seriously. In general, in mainstreaming activities there appears to be an emphasis on adaptation rather than on both adaptation and mitigation, e.g. GEF projects such as Mainstreaming Adaptation to Climate Change in the Caribbean (MACC, 2006).

We refer to Bizikova et al. (2007) for a more extensive discussion on the integration of climate change considerations in decision-making at the local level, creating partnerships between local authorities, citizens' groups, the private sector and scientists, and building capacity to effectively respond to climate change.

6. Discussion and recommendations

Mitigation and adaptation have been separated, to some extent artificially, in science as well as policy. The reasons for this have been discussed above. Since there is now general agreement that climate change is unavoidable and that unmitigated climate change may lead to serious impacts for natural ecosystems and human society, the question is not whether the climate has to be protected from humans or humans from climate, but how both mitigation and adaptation can be pursued in tandem. It may be tempting to now reduce the emphasis on the individual strategies and call for integrated responses that are based on optimal, least-cost solutions. Our analysis suggests that integrated approaches can indeed provide very promising options, which can primarily be identified in those sectors that can play a major role in both mitigation and adaptation, notably land-use and urban planning, agriculture and forestry, and water management. However, in some sectors, the balance of adaptation and mitigation benefits can be very uncertain. For example, in urban design, increased cooling needs and climate-friendly siting have effects which work in different directions. In the energy sector, renewable energy can reduce GHG emissions but increase vulnerability of supply. In practice, to our knowledge, few opportunities for synergistic action are yet captured, because of low awareness. However, the majority of mitigation options in key sectors such as energy, transport, buildings, industry and waste do not have any clear link with climate change adaptation, and hence the synergetic options appear to be limited in scope from a global perspective.

We have argued that the costs and benefits of climate change are too widely distributed over disparate actors and geographical and temporal scales, and uncertainties relating to costs of mitigation, adaptation and residual impacts are too large to find a meaningful answer to the question of what the most efficient and cheapest combination of adaptation and mitigation policies would be. Rather, it may be more relevant and urgent to broaden the menu of usually parallel mitigation and adaptation options and to broaden the analysis of their linkages. We propose the following five ways to develop linked adaptation and mitigation strategies:

1. *Avoid trade-offs*: when designing adaptation options, their consequences for mitigation should be routinely taken into account and vice versa, something that can be facilitated by including such considerations in the available methodological toolkits, such as design criteria and project cost–benefit analyses.
2. *Identify synergies*: for specific sectoral climate response options, notably in those sectors mentioned above, those options can be identified that contribute to both reduced greenhouse gas emissions and reduced vulnerability to climate change.
3. *Enhance and apply response capacity*: since the determinants of adaptive and mitigative capacity largely overlap, strengthening these determinants in developing countries contributes to both; in industrialized countries the emphasis should be on putting the existing capacity into action.
4. *Develop institutional links*: between adaptation and mitigation, where they are currently missing: mechanisms should be put in place to enhance communication between mitigation and adaptation policy-makers and explore innovative links, e.g. at the national level, but also in the UNFCCC negotiations, where linking adaptation and mitigation may help in bridging differences between countries.
5. *Mainstreaming*: both greenhouse gas emissions and vulnerability to climate change are as much dependent on non-climate policies as on climate policies; therefore it would be wise to integrate climate change mitigation and adaptation considerations into all general development policies. This is important for mitigation as well as adaptation, in developed as well as in developing countries.

Acknowledgement

The authors thank two anonymous reviewers for their useful comments.

Notes

1. One may wonder how climate policy would have developed if the early definitional split between mitigation and adaptation had not occurred. In health care, both types of response are captured by a single term: prevention.
2. Some definitions and examples: *risk* = probability * impact; *impact*: e.g. damage in US$, loss in life years, in crop yield, in species diversity; *climate change hazard*: e.g. in ΔT, Δprecipitation; *exposure*: e.g. number of people, area of crop land or ecosystem exposed; *sensitivity*: e.g. $I/\Delta T/cap$, $I/\Delta T/ha$; *adaptive capacity*: e.g. in % potential impact reduction; *potential impacts* = exposure * sensitivity; *vulnerability* = potential impact/adaptive capacity.
3. It is worth mentioning that reducing particulate matter emissions not only reduces detrimental health effects but also lessens the aerosol cooling effect of these emissions.
4. At the national level, costs of mitigation are generally estimated to be relatively low, generally less than a few percent of GDP, which is equivalent to a small decrease in the GDP growth rate, dependent on the level and timing of emissions reductions. For specific sectors, societal groups or regions this can be different. An example of the latter would be that income growth lowered by mitigation policies may actually at some point increase the incidence of malaria morbidity and mortality (Tol and Dowlatabadi, 2001).
5. An earlier table was expanded by including ideas from a similar matrix in Bizikova et al. (2006).

References

Agrawala, S. (ed.), 2005, *Bridge Over Troubled Waters: Linking Climate Change and Development*, OECD, Paris.

Banuri, T., Weyant, J., 2001, 'Setting the stage: climate change and sustainable development', in: B. Metz, O. Davidson, J. Pan, R. Swart (eds), *Climate Change 2001: Mitigation*, IPCC Third Assessment Report, Cambridge University Press, Cambridge, UK.

Bizikova, L., Burch, S., Cohen, S., Robinson, J., 2006, *Climate Change and Sustainable Development in the Local Context: Linking Research and Policy*, Background Paper International Workshop on Climate Change Adaptation, Mitigation and Linkages with Sustainable Development.

Bizikova, L., Robinson, J., Cohen, S., 2007, 'Linking climate change and sustainable development at the local level', *Climate Policy* 7(4), 271–277.

Burton, I., van Aalst, M., 2004, *Look Before You Leap: A Risk Management Approach for Incorporating Climate Change Adaptation into World Bank Operations*, World Bank, Washington, DC.

Dang, H.H., Michaelowa, A., Tuan, D.D., 2003, 'Synergy of adaptation and mitigation strategies in the context of sustainable development: the case of Vietnam', *Climate Policy* 3(S1), S81–S96.

EC (European Commission), 2001, *A Sustainable Europe for a Better World: A European Union Strategy for Sustainable Development*, COM(2001)264 final, European Commission, Brussels.

EC (European Commission), 2005, *Winning the Battle Against Global Climate Change*, COM(2005)35 final, European Commission, Brussels.

EC (European Commission), 2007a, *Limiting Global Climate Change to 2 Degrees Celsius: The Way Ahead for 2020 and Beyond*, {SEC(2007) 7/8}, European Commission, Brussels.

EC (European Commission), 2007b, *Adapting to Climate Change in Europe: Options for EU Action*, {SEC(2007) 849}, European Commission, Brussels.

Fearnside, P.M., 2006, 'Greenhouse gas emissions from hydroelectric dams: reply to Rosa et al.', *Climatic Change* 75(1–2), 91–102.

Huq, S., Rahman, A., Konate, M., Sokona, Y., Reid, H., 2003, *Mainstreaming Adaptation to Climate Change in Least Developed Countries*, International Institute for Environment and Development (IIED), London.

IPCC, 2001, *Climate Change 2001: Synthesis Report*, Cambridge University Press, Cambridge, UK.

IPCC, 2007, *Climate Change 2007: Mitigation*, Cambridge University Press, Cambridge, UK.

Jones, R., 2006, *Risk Management: Approaches and Methods*, DIW Berlin Cost of Inaction Workshop, Berlin.

Kane, S., Shogren, J.F., 2000, 'Linking adaptation and mitigation in climate change policy', *Climatic Change* 45, 75–101.

Klein, R., Schipper, E.L.F., Dessai, S., 2005, 'Integrating mitigation and adaptation into climate and development policy: three research questions', *Environmental Science and Policy* 8, 579–588.

MACC (Mainstreaming Adaptation to Climate Change in the Caribbean), 2006, *Mainstreaming Adaptation to Climate Change: Project Overview* [available at www.oas.org/macc/].

Michaelowa, A., 2001, *Mitigation versus Adaptation: The Political Economy of Competition between Climate Policy Strategies and the Consequences for Developing Countries*, HWWA Discussion Paper No. 153, Hamburg, Germany.

Munasinghe, M., Swart, R., 2004, *Primer on Climate Change and Sustainable Development: Facts, Policy Analysis and Applications*, Cambridge University Press, Cambridge, UK.

Peltonen, L., Haanpää, S., Lehtonen, S., 2005, *The Challenge of Climate Change Adaptation in Urban Planning*, FINADAPT Working Paper 13, Finnish Environment Institute Mimeographs 343, Helsinki.

Pielke, R.A., 1998, 'Rethinking the role of adaptation in climate policy', *Global Environmental Change* 8(2), 159–170.

Pielke, R.A., 2004, 'What is climate change? Incompatibility between the definitions used by science and policy organizations is an obstacle to effective action', *Issues in Science and Technology* 20(4), 31 [available at http://sciencepolicy.colorado.edu/admin/publication_files/resource-486-2004.09.pdf].

Rosa, L.P., Dos Santos, M.A., Matvienko, B., Sikar, E., Dos Santos, E.O., 2006, 'Scientific errors in the Fearnside comments on greenhouse gas emissions (GHG) from hydroelectric dams and response to his political claiming', *Climatic Change* 75(1–2), 91–102.

Sheltair, 2003, *A Sustainable Urban System: The Long-Term Plan for Greater Vancouver*, Sheltair Group, Vancouver, Canada.

Stern, N., 2006, *The Economics of Climate Change*, The Stern Review, Cabinet Office–HM Treasury/Cambridge University Press, Cambridge, UK.

Tol, R., 2005, 'Adaptation and mitigation: trade-offs in substance and methods', *Environmental Science and Policy* 8, 572–578.

Tol, R., 2006, 'Exchange rates and climate change: an application of FUND', *Climatic Change* 75(1–2), 59–80.

Tol, R.S.J., Dowlatabadi, H., 2001, 'Vector-borne diseases, climate change, and economic growth', *Integrated Assessment* 2, 173–181.

Tompkins, E.L., Adger, W.N., 2005, 'Defining response capacity to enhance climate change policy', *Environmental Science and Policy* 8, 562–571.

Toth, F.L., Mwandosya, M., Carraro, C., Christensen, J., Edmonds, J., Flannery, B., Gay-Garcia, C., Lee, H., Meyer-Abich, K.M., Nikitina, E., Rhaman, A., Richels, R., Ye, R., Villavicencio, A., Wake, Y., Weyant, J., 2001, 'Decision-making frameworks', in: B. Metz, O. Davidson, R. Swart, J. Pan (eds), *Climate Change 2001: Mitigation*, Intergovernmental Panel on Climate Change, Cambridge University Press, Cambridge, UK.

UNFCCC, 1992, *United Nations Framework Convention on Climate Change*.

UNFCCC (United Framework Conference on Climate Change), 2002, *The Delhi Ministerial Declaration on Climate Change and Sustainable Development*.

UNFCCC (United Framework Conference on Climate Change), 2006, *Five-year Programme of Work of the Subsidiary Body for Scientific and Technological Advice on Impacts, Vulnerability and Adaptation to Climate Change*, Decision 2/CP.11, FCCC/CP/2005/5/Add.1

Wilbanks, T.J., 2005, 'Issues in developing a capacity for integrated analysis of mitigation and adaptation', *Environmental Science and Policy* 8, 541–547.

Wilbanks, T.J., 2007, 'Scale and sustainability', *Climate Policy* 7(4), 278–287.

Wilbanks, T.J., Kane, S.M., Leiby, P.N., Perlack, R.D., Settle, C., Shogren, J.F., Smith, J.B., 2003, 'Integrating mitigation and adaptation: possible responses to global climate change', *Environment* 45(5), 28–38.

Winkler, H., Baumert, K., Blanchard, O., Burch, S., Robinson, J., 2007, 'What factors influence mitigative capacity', *Energy Policy* 35, 692–703.

World Commission on Dams, 2000, *Workshop on Dam Reservoirs and Greenhouse Gases (Part III)*, Hydro-Quebec, Montreal, Canada.

Yohe, G., 2006, 'On the complementary role of mitigation and adaptation at a local level given uncertain climate change', in: L. Bizikova, S. Cohen (eds), *Final Report of the International Workshop on Climate Change Adaptation, Mitigation and Linkages with Sustainable Development*. Institute for Resources Environment and Sustainability, University of British Columbia, Canada.

Yohe, G., Toth, F.L., 2000, 'Adaptation and the guardrail approach to tolerable climate change', *Climate Change* 45(7), 103–128.

synthesis article

A framework for explaining the links between capacity and action in response to global climate change

SARAH BURCH*, JOHN ROBINSON

Institute for Resources, Environment, and Sustainability (IRES), University of British Columbia, 2202 Main Mall, Vancouver, British Columbia, Canada, V6T 1Z4

Although great strides have been made towards a more nuanced understanding of the impacts and causes of global climate change, the ability to design and implement policy responses that engender effective action has remained insufficient. Recent framings of adaptive capacity and mitigative capacity are built upon in this article, and response capacity is introduced as a useful way to integrate adaptation and mitigation within the context of underlying development paths. In tracing the complex and non-linear relationships between response capacity – which represents a broad pool of development-related resources that can be mobilized in the face of any risk – and real policy and behaviour change in response to climate change, the strong influence of manifold socio-cultural factors is revealed. Only through an analysis of these deeper trajectories can the most important barriers to action begin to be addressed. Theories of risk perception are drawn upon to elucidate the complex nature of the relationship between capacity and action. A deeper understanding of these relationships will aid in the design and implementation of adaptation and mitigation policies that more effectively address the multitude of temporally and contextually specific intricacies of human behaviour in response to risks such as climate change. The literatures of institutional genesis and change, socio-technical systems, social movements, and collective behaviour change theory (to name but a few) are argued to be crucial to an improved understanding of the underlying development paths which influence both capacity and action.

Keywords: adaptive capacity; climate change; development paths; mitigative capacity; policy formation; socio-technical contexts; sustainable development

Bien que de gros progrès aient été faits vers une compréhension plus nuancée des causes et impacts du changement climatique global, l'aptitude à concevoir et mettre en place les réponses politiques pour une action véritable est cependant restée insuffisante jusqu'ici. Cet article élabore les structures récentes, et le thème de la capacité de réponse en tant que manière pratique d'intégrer adaptation et mitigation dans le contexte de scénarios de développement sous-jacents est introduit. En traçant les liens complexes et non-linéaires entre, d'une part, les capacités de réponse, représentant un large groupement de ressources liées au développement qui pourraient être mobilisées face à n'importe quel risque, et, d'autre part, les vrais changements des politiques et des comportements face au changement climatique, la forte influence de multiples facteurs socioculturels est révélée. C'est uniquement à travers l'analyse de ces trajectoires profondes que les principaux obstacles à l'action peuvent être abordées. Nous nous appuyons sur les théories sur la perception du risque pour élucider la nature complexe des liens entre capacité et action. Une compréhension plus profonde de ces liens aidera dans la conception et la mise en place de politiques d'adaptation et de mitigation à même de mieux aborder la multitude de complexités d'ordre temporel et contextuel des comportements humain face à aux risques tels que le changement climatique. Nous avançons que la littérature sur la genèse institutionnelle et le changement, les systèmes technico-sociaux, les mouvements sociaux, et la théorie sur les changements de comportement de groupes sont essentiels parmi bien d'autres à l'améliorération de la connaissance des scénarios de développement sous-jacents à même d'influencer la capacité ainsi que l'action.

Mots clés: capacités d'adaptation; capacités de mitigation; changement du climat; contextes technico-sociaux; développement durable; élaboration de politiques; scenarios de développement

■ *Corresponding author. E-mail*: sburch@interchange.ubc.ca

CLIMATE POLICY **7 (2007) 304–316**

© 2007 Earthscan ISSN: 1469-3062 (print), 1752-7457 (online) www.climatepolicy.com

1. Introduction

Since the mid 1990s, the enhanced greenhouse effect and global climate change have become issues around which much public debate has centred. Initially, this debate was characterized by heated discussions regarding the precision and relevance of temperature and impacts models, even periodically calling into question the most fundamental assumptions of climate scientists. More recently, dramatic shifts have occurred within the climate change discourse itself, quite separately from the increased prominence of climate change as a political issue in jurisdictions around the world. First, perhaps partly because of the difficulty of regulating climate change at the global level, many scholars are beginning to consider the implications of climate change at ever smaller scales. Local and regional responses to climate change, such as the US Mayors Climate Protection Agreement, have become more common in the time since the negotiation of the Kyoto Protocol to the United Nations Framework Convention on Climate Change (Wilbanks and Kates, 1999; Betsill, 2001; Jones et al., 2007).

Second, novel efforts are being made to link previously disparate categories of climate change responses, such as adaptation and mitigation, within a framework of sustainable development (see Bizikova et al., 2007). This new approach will assist in the development of local-level climate response strategies that consider inevitable trade-offs, and potentially attractive synergies, between responses that may influence the ability of a collective to follow a sustainable development path.

Finally, increasing attention is being given to the underlying characteristics of a society which either help or hinder responses to climate change (Sagar, 2000; Adger et al., 2003; Brooks et al., 2005; Haddad, 2005; Tompkins and Adger, 2005). Especially important to these discussions is the concept of capacity, and its influence on action in response to climate change. It is this issue that this article addresses in detail, with the goal of further elaborating the nature of the complex relationship between capacity and action. To this end, the networks of interactions that connect a group's underlying development path with the resultant mitigation and adaptation are considered, and important factors that mediate these interactions are identified. Specifically, theories of risk perception are drawn upon to provide insights into just one of the many socio-cultural patterns that will influence our ability to address the risks associated with climate change.

2. Capacity and the climate change problem

A central component of recent discussions regarding the human dimensions of climate change is the concept of capacity. This section introduces adaptive and mitigative capacity. The evolution of these concepts within the climate community is considered, and a way in which adaptive and mitigative capacity can be more carefully defined to assist in the explication of the links between capacity and action in response to climate change is proposed. Finally, this section introduces response capacity as a useful idea through which adaptation and mitigation can be integrated in the context of sustainable development.

2.1 Adaptive and mitigative capacity

As the science of climate change risk becomes more established, and greater consensus is reached among climate system experts around the world, attention has shifted to the issue of responding to climate change. Responses are typically grouped into two categories: climate change mitigation, which reduces emissions or increases the capture of greenhouse gases in order to reduce the magnitude of the future risk; and adaptation, which consists of adjustments in structures, practices or processes, in order to respond to changing climate conditions (IPCC, 2001a). Recent literature in the field of climate change response argues that adaptation to, and mitigation of, climate change take place within the context of adaptive and mitigative capacity, respectively (Yohe, 2001; Brooks et al., 2005; Tompkins and Adger, 2005). This article takes as its starting point the definitions proposed by the IPCC Fourth Assessment Report (IPCC, 2001a), which defines adaptive capacity as 'the ability or potential of a system to respond successfully to climate variability and change' (Adger et al., 2007). We adopt a more recent definition of mitigative capacity, which describes it as the ability to reduce greenhouse gas emissions that lead to global climate change (Winkler et al., 2007).

The concept of capacity only emerged with the IPCC's Third Assessment Report, and was a significant development in the path towards a more nuanced explication of responses to climate change. Prior to the Third Assessment Report, most analyses of human responses to climate change were limited to estimations of specific climate change impacts and proposals for mitigation and adaptation responses, rather than investigations into the socio-political and institutional precursors to these responses. This focus was established in the First and Second Assessment Reports of the Intergovernmental Panel on Climate Change (IPCC)[1], a collaborative effort between the United Nations Environment Programme (UNEP) and the World Meteorological Organization (WMO). Published in 1991 and 1995, these reports captured the focus of the research on climate change that had taken place during the preceding decade, and dealt intensively with issues of modelling the potential impacts of anthropogenic climate change, greenhouse gas reduction through mitigation, and issues of the cost-effectiveness or efficiency of mitigation policies (Banuri et al., 2001). This reflected the natural science-driven and somewhat technocratic views of the climate change community at the time (Cohen et al., 1998). The assumption was made that science could be used to fill the knowledge gaps that plagued studies of climate change, and that policy makers could simply rationally apply this knowledge to the development and implementation of effective response strategies (Irwin, 1995; Irwin and Wynne, 1996; Jasanoff and Wynne, 1998). A recognition of the limits of this approach led to an attempt by the IPCC, in the Third and Fourth Assessment Reports, to pay significantly more attention to questions about the need for consideration of more human issues, such as the social, cultural, political or institutional constraints on responses to climate change (Banuri et al., 2001; Smit et al., 2001). An example of this new focus was the introduction of the concept of adaptive and mitigative capacity in the Third Assessment Report (Banuri et al., 2001; Smit et al., 2001), and the increasingly integrated treatment of the inter-relationships between adaptation and mitigation in the Fourth Assessment Report (Klein et al., 2007). Even after this introduction occurred, however, the research response within the climate change community remained limited. As such, the concept of capacity, and its implications for climate change mitigation and adaptation, is only now emerging into prominence.

In arenas other than that of traditionally natural-science-dominated climate change research, however, the question of capacity for behaviour change has been investigated extensively. Early framing of the climate change problem, embodied in the first two assessment reports of the IPCC, underestimated the contributions of social sciences such as cultural anthropology, sociology and social psychology to 'understanding the processes by which societies recognize new threats to their security or well-being, formulate responses, and act collectively upon them' (Jasanoff and Wynne, 1998). Some have argued that, in the arena of climate change, the rather unsettled relationship between the natural and social sciences arises out of the very different epistemological roots from which these disciplines grew. The traditional, natural-science-based climate change discourse was somewhat reductionist in nature, attempted to mould the climate change problem to suit the requirements of scientific analysis, and mostly ignored the political, social and cultural dimensions of the problem (Cohen et al., 1998). The human-centred social science discourse, on the other hand, sought to explain the drivers of climate change in a more politically sensitive and geographically appropriate manner, but was often considered to be analytically vague by more quantitatively oriented scholars (Cohen et al., 1998). It is out of this more human-centred approach that the concepts of adaptive and mitigative capacity have arisen.

The concept of adaptive capacity was first brought to the attention of the climate change community because of its use in the field of ecology (Hawley, 1986). The ability of a system to withstand and adapt to external stresses had long been a subject of study in the scientific community, but the resilience of human communities and economic systems was not initially part of this analysis. Over the last several decades, however, a large literature has developed that investigates adaptive human responses in the realm of ecosystem management (see, for example, Holling, 1978; Holling, 1986; Berkes et al., 2000a, 2000b; Yohe, 2001; Folke et al., 2002). These elements were eventually added to the consideration of adaptive capacity in the climate change community, and articulated by Yohe (2001). Yohe suggested that adaptive capacity was determined by the following group-level characteristics:

- the range of available technological options for adaptation
- the availability of resources and their distribution across the population
- the structure of critical institutions and the derivative allocation of decision-making authority
- the stock of human capital, including education and personal security
- the stock of social capital including the definition of property rights
- the system's access to risk-spreading processes
- the ability of decision makers to manage information, the processes by which these decision makers determine which information is credible, and the credibility of the decision makers themselves
- the public perception of attribution (Yohe, 2001).

In parallel to adaptive capacity, mitigative capacity refers to the ability of a system to undertake climate change mitigation. It is typically human-centred, but is connected to natural systems through the accumulation of carbon in these systems, and is determined by a variety of characteristics of the socio-technical system within which mitigation takes place. The work of Gary Yohe (2001) again assisted in the initial elucidation of these determinants, and posited that essentially the same set of characteristics helps to determine the mitigative response to climate change (Yohe, 2001). Yohe adds that acknowledgement of the determinants of both adaptive and mitigative capacity may lead to more effective research and policies to deal with responses to the climate change risk (Yohe, 2001). The wide acceptability of the hypotheses put forward by Yohe is demonstrated by their integration in the Third and Fourth Assessment Reports of the Intergovernmental Panel on Climate Change (IPCC) (IPCC, 2001a, 2001b; Klein et al., 2007; Sathaye et al., 2007), and their reiteration and further development by numerous climate change experts (Moss et al., 2001; Adger et al., 2004). A more integrated approach to the analysis of adaptation and mitigation is currently gaining momentum, leading to preliminary policy recommendations (Jones et al., 2007; Winkler et al., 2007).

2.2 Response capacity

As outlined above, recent research supports the view of Yohe that adaptive capacity and mitigative capacity are essentially driven by the same factors (Tompkins and Adger, 2005). These factors, or determinants, however, operate at a very high level of abstraction and seem to apply only to very large groups. Furthermore, these determinants yield little insight into crucial aspects of climate responses; namely: what party is initiating the response action, and how is that action carried out? In other words, more information is required about the institution or agency, and the resultant policies and programmes, which are geared towards adaptive and mitigative responses to climate change, if the factors that engender effective and ineffective climate change responses are to be articulated.

For these reasons, it may be fruitful to consider the broad determinants of capacity, as outlined by Yohe and others, to be part of a more general, development-related, pool of resources called 'response capacity'. A slightly different framing of the term 'response capacity' has been proposed by Tompkins and Adger (2005), who suggested that response capacity can be thought of as the human ability to manage both the generation of greenhouse gases and the consequences of their production (Tompkins and Adger, 2005). Put differently, response capacity, according to this framing, represents simply the confluence of adaptive and mitigative capacity. This concept may be broadened, however, in order to represent the broad pool of resources that can be utilized to address any risk or challenge faced by a human society. The value of this broadening is that it allows response capacity to be connected to the underlying socio-economic and technological development path of a given society or community and thus provides a new focus for our attempts to understand how capacity can effectively be translated into action.

Response capacity, according to this view, is time- and context-specific, and culturally and regionally specific. It consists of a broad set of resources, many of which have previously been described as the determinants of adaptive and mitigative capacity. For instance, stocks of human and social capital, which are pools of resources that may be used in a multitude of ways, are elements of response capacity. In addition, the presence of technological innovation and economic strength of a nation contribute to its store of response capacity. As a result, response capacity is to some extent an approximation of a nation's development level, and thus is rooted in a nation's development path.

On the surface, the concept of response capacity may appear to represent a further step towards the analytical vagueness that has plagued the concepts of mitigative and adaptive capacity in the past. Response capacity, however, draws our attention to a very important set of processes and dynamic interactions between various technological, institutional and cultural trajectories which are fundamentally rooted in the underlying development path. In other words, the resources which contribute to response capacity represent potentially path-dependent systems of rules, institutional structures, and habitual practices, which may be the precursors of significant barriers to action. As we shall see, these underlying institutional, socio-technical and cultural trajectories fundamentally constrain the ways that mitigative and adaptive capacity play out in practice. Thus, the concept of response capacity simultaneously allows for the greater specification of mitigative and adaptive capacity, and reveals the importance of deeper socio-cultural trajectories that form the context within which action may occur. The examples of the interrelationships between response capacity, adaptive capacity and mitigative capacity that are discussed in this section serve to illustrate this claim.

The generalized pools of resources that constitute response capacity might be utilized to produce an institution or policy that is geared towards mitigation of, or adaptation to, climate change, which represents the formation of adaptive and/or mitigative capacity out of the pool of response capacity resources. For instance, generalized institutional capacity, in the form of government budgetary capacity and jurisdiction, might be activated in the creation of an agency or institution that is geared towards carrying out emergency measures in response to severe climate events. Similarly, a Corporate Social Responsibility or environmental division of a large corporation might be formulated out of pre-existing institutional capacity and human capital, which then goes on to design effective policies geared towards the reduction of greenhouse gas emissions. In this case, it is unlikely that the embodiment of response capacity in a form of adaptive capacity will do much to build or enhance mitigative capacity. Similarly, the presence of technological innovation that has grown out of a socio-technical system might result in technologies that are applicable only to the reduction of greenhouse gas emissions, but contribute nothing to the adaptation to climate change impacts. This clearly implies that trade-offs may exist in the way that general response capacities are transformed into more specific mitigative or adaptive capacities. For example, to the extent that climate change policy responses in general have available to them only a finite amount of resources within a given governmental policy framework, then adaptive and mitigative measures may compete for these resources even if they are not substitutes in terms of their effects.

Two important dimensions of the relationship between response capacity and adaptive/mitigative capacities require further elaboration, and speak to the fact that response capacity resources may be manifested in a form of mitigative capacity that has implications for adaptation, or a form of adaptive capacity that influences mitigation goals. First, once response capacity is transformed into either mitigative capacity or adaptive capacity, it may or may not serve the other function. For instance, response capacity in the form of human and financial capital, which may contribute to the development of alternative energy technologies, can be instantiated in the form of an agency and policies geared towards decentralized renewable energy generation. This is more likely to result in cases where fewer technological, economic and institutional path dependencies exist in the energy system, which arises out of the underlying development path. Although not the driving purpose of such an agency and its policies, this form of mitigative capacity also has important implications for adaptive capacity insofar as it enhances resilience and diminishes the vulnerability associated with centralized power generation. In this way, the instantiation of response capacity in the form of mitigative capacity yields unintended benefits for adaptive capacity as well. Similarly, resources that are part of response capacity may be utilized to produce a municipal agency with the mandate of designing and implementing sustainable urban growth or densification policies. One aspect of these policies might be the design of urban forms that simultaneously consume less energy than current forms, reduce storm-water runoff and the resulting need for water treatment, and lead to urban systems that are more adaptable to climate extremes and energy security issues. In this way, response capacity has been transformed into an agency which embodies both adaptive and mitigative capacity.

Trade-offs may also exist in the translation of response capacity into adaptive and mitigative capacity. For instance, response capacity may be utilized to form a flood protection and dyke management agency, geared explicitly towards implementing adaptation measures. This is likely in an area that has accumulated technical expertise to deal with such issues, constructed an institutional framework to support these actions, and entrenched flood protection responses in a system of policies and mandates. Not only does this likely take resources away from mitigation-oriented measures, but the construction and management of dykes will be likely to consume the fossil fuels that actually contribute to the climate change problem (and thus the need for mitigation). Again, it is clear that the underlying technological, institutional and socio-cultural trajectories fundamentally shape the way that response capacity is transformed into mitigative and adaptive capacities, as well as into action. Recent work on the part of climate-change scholars has begun to explore a more comprehensive framework for the consideration of interactions between adaptation and mitigation, as well as their respective capacities (Beg et al., 2002; Dang et al., 2003; Wilbanks and Sathaye, 2007; Wilbanks et al., 2007; Yohe and Strzepek, 2007). It is clear that the ways in which response capacity is transformed into adaptive and mitigative capacity are manifold, creating layers of interaction leading to very different climate response outcomes.

The relationships among response capacity, mitigative and adaptive capacities, and actual mitigation and adaptation proposed here are illustrated in Figure 1. First, the schematic shows that all factors that contribute to human responses to climate change are embedded in the underlying development path. In other words, socio-cultural, technological and institutional trajectories fundamentally shape the quality and quantity of response capacity resources, which are then available for mitigative and adaptive activities. Next, adaptive and mitigative capacity are shown to arise out of these response capacity resources, in the form of institutions and policies

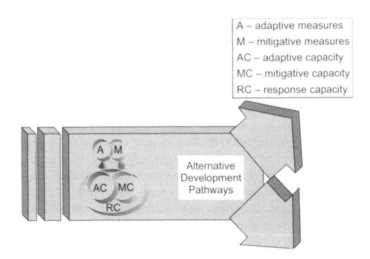

A – adaptive measures
M – mitigative measures
AC – adaptive capacity
MC – mitigative capacity
RC – response capacity

Alternative
Development
Pathways

FIGURE 1 The process of transformation of response capacity, which is a generalized set of resources rooted in the development path, into mitigative and adaptive capacity, and finally into action (mitigation and adaptation)

that are geared towards one or both of these responses. Finally, adaptive and mitigative capacities are utilized to produce adaptation or mitigation in response to the climate change risk.

3. Translating capacity into action

The discussion above, which provides a proposed clarification of the concepts of response capacity, and adaptive and mitigative capacity, lays the groundwork for addressing the central question, often left unasked, with regard to human responses to climate change: does a group with larger stocks of capacity necessarily respond more effectively than a group with less? More generally, one must ask: what influences the relationship between capacity and action? This section first considers criticisms of, and additions to, the traditional formulation of the determinants of adaptive and mitigative capacity, which provide the roots of the capacity/action question. Next, the translation of capacity into action is considered, and one important factor which may shape this relationship is introduced.

Although the determinants of capacity, as laid out by Gary Yohe, have come to be widely accepted in the IPCC and global climate research circles, recent work has suggested that Yohe's list of determinants is incomplete. Haddad (2005), for instance, suggests that the traditional measures of adaptive capacity do not consider the normative or motivational context of adaptation. Specifically, Haddad examines the effect of national goals and aspirations on adaptation choices. Teleological legitimacy, procedural legitimacy, and norm-based decision rules are three broad categories of goals that Haddad argues might lead nations to make different decisions in response to the climate change risk (Haddad, 2005). Although he deals specifically with adaptation and makes no claims about the effects of national aspirations on mitigative responses to climate change, one might argue that the motivational context behind mitigation is equally important. But from the point of view of the approach taken in this article, these factors have more to do with the process of turning capacity into action than with expanding the list of determinants of capacity.

Grothmann and Patt (2005) stress the need for an examination of responses to climate change that, instead of considering resource constraints as the most significant determinant of adaptation, separates out the psychological steps that precede action in response to perception of the climate change risk. A large literature pertaining to human decision making and action, traditionally outside of the climate change realm, suggests that both motivation and perceived abilities are important determinants of action (Dietz et al., 1998; Stern, 2000; Kollmuss and Agyeman, 2002). Thus, both risk perception and perceived adaptive capacity, for instance, may enhance or inhibit adaptive responses to climate change (Grothmann and Patt, 2005).

These criticisms of, and additions to, Yohe's determinants of adaptive and mitigative capacity point to the need to revise the previously deterministic view of capacity and action, and to consider more carefully the intricacies of human behaviour. They suggest the need to relate adaptive and mitigative capacity to the concrete institutional and socio-technological contexts in which these capacities are embedded. To the extent that these capacities are part of a trajectory of decisions and behaviours that prioritize or even make conceivable only certain forms of action, then proposals for policy responses that are incompatible with such a trajectory are much less likely to succeed or even be seriously considered.

An example of such path dependence might be policy regimes that subscribe to a strongly market-oriented approach to policy formation. In such regimes, response capacity is much more easily mobilized for forms of adaptive or mitigative responses that reflect such priorities (e.g. market-based instruments) than for forms of response characterized by more traditional command-and-control policies. In this way, the development pathway may strongly condition the types of responses considered legitimate.

Although the adaptive and mitigative capacity literature does not claim that building capacity will necessarily lead to improved responses to the climate change risk, little work has been done to explicate the widely noted variation in response to climate change among communities and nations with similar capacities. For instance, Canada and Sweden are remarkably similar according to a variety of economic, demographic and geographical indicators. Canada's GDP per capita is US$29,000 (US 2004 dollars), while Sweden's is US$26,000 per capita, Canada and Sweden face similar northern hemisphere climates, and are currently passing through similar stages of their demographic transitions, marked by aging populations and slow growth (CIA, 2004). Canada and Sweden also possess similarly high literacy rates, similar distributions of GDP by sector, and so on. These two nations are exposed to the same internationally endorsed climate change science, through the IPCC, and have access to essentially the same mitigative and adaptive technologies via open markets and international trade. Such similarities indicate that Canada and Sweden possess very similar levels of response capacity. These two countries, however, have very different levels and types of climate-change-related institutions and policies (adaptive and mitigative capacity), and very different success in reducing greenhouse gas emissions. Canada, despite having ratified the Kyoto Protocol, has experienced a 24.2% increase in emissions since 1990, while Sweden has managed to reduce its emissions by 2.3% (UNFCCC, 2005). This variation in response and the potential influence of varying perceptions of risk reveal that capacity is a necessary, but not sufficient, condition for mitigative action (Winkler et al., 2007). Clearly, additional factors are influencing the complex and non-linear relationship between response capacity and behaviour change.

In order to tease out some characteristics of the relationship between capacity and action in climate change, one factor – risk perception – will be provided as an example of a context-specific, culturally variable factor that may play some role in the variance in climate change responses among countries.

4. Example: Risk perception and varying responses to climate change

Studies of the perception of risk offer considerable insight into common patterns of behaviour that individuals and groups might follow in response to a risk such as climate change. Although most of the work in this area has been carried out to explain technological disasters (such as chemical spills or nuclear disasters) or, more strictly, natural disasters (such as an earthquake or a tsunami), this literature has much to offer any explanation of nations' or groups' policy responses to climate change. Research dealing with the perception and characterization of risk can be grouped into two approaches: psychological or psychometric, and socio-cultural. Each of these will be addressed below.

Although scientific experts have often considered the responses of policy makers and the lay public to risk to be irrational, key scholars in the sub-field of psychological or psychometric studies of risk perception argue otherwise (Wynne, 1992; Kempton, 1997; Lowe et al., 2006). Rather than responding to some 'true' level of risk that is inherent in changing climate, this literature posits that the lay public creates perceptions of risk that are based on different criteria and thus may differ from those of the experts. These perceptions are still rational, however, and are based on two factors, each of which is made up of a combination of characteristics (Slovic, 1992). In particular, these scholars posit that perceptions of risk are derived essentially from feelings of dread (resulting from a risk that is perceived to be severe, catastrophic or uncontrollable), and the unknown (often resulting from risks that are perceived to be unfamiliar, unobservable or new to science) (Slovic, 1992). These perceptions are individual, however, and are therefore strongly affected by the socio-economic standing of the individual perceiving the risk. It has been found, for instance, that economically and socially disadvantaged populations, such as visible minorities and women, are likely to perceive risks to be greater than their more empowered counterparts (Satterfield et al., 2004). These disadvantaged groups possess much less power in their socio-political surroundings, and thus have less reason to believe that they can control or recover from a risk. It has often been noted that less-wealthy and minority communities are less likely to receive protection from harm (Bullard, 1994), and are more likely to be located in environmentally unstable or unsafe locations, such as cliffs or low-lying areas prone to flooding and inundation. Climate change may prove to be a very real risk to these groups, who, as the victims of environmental injustice, are least likely to be well served by the political and economic services that are at the disposal of others. Thus, the groups that have the highest concerns about risks related to climate change may be least empowered to translate those concerns into policy, leading to a systematic under-representation of risk concerns.

Risks related to climate change are especially susceptible to variation in perception, in part because of the scientific controversy discussed previously and in part because of the geographical variation in vulnerability, provision of scientific information, and economic stability. As such, a community (Group A) that is economically resilient, with few marginalized groups, high education and literacy levels, and minimal risk of extreme exposure to the impacts of climate change, might associate low levels of dread and 'unknowability' with climate change. This group might perceive the risk of climate change to be relatively minor, thereby carrying out few adaptation or mitigation options. Group B, on the other hand, might be characterized by groups that are economically or socially disadvantaged, privy to conflicting information about the potential risks of climate change, and physically vulnerable. This group, according to Slovic's psychometric factor space, would perceive the risks from climate change to be much greater. If this group possesses considerable response capacity, then it may be more likely to carry out adaptive or mitigative actions. One could easily imagine communities with a mixture of these characteristics as well. For instance, Group C might be highly vulnerable (for instance a low-lying Small Island State), leading to high estimations of the severity and fatality of climate change, but might also consider climate change to be a familiar and observable risk. Group D, alternatively, experiences low levels of dread in relation to the climate change risk, but regards climate change as a mysterious and unobservable force that is unknown and new to science. The levels of mitigation in these latter, more ambiguous, groups might depend more strongly on other factors such as political structures, political will, and capacity.

The groups described above, however, clearly represent idealized versions of reality. Since most jurisdictions consist of mixtures of these groups, power and representation become the resources that most directly influence the responses of a group to climate change. For instance, the risk perception of the less-empowered majority may not be the risk perception that characterizes the more affluent or empowered minority. As a result, the response of the group as a whole may be far from representative of the majority.

Social theories of risk also lend considerable insight into variation in perceptions of the climate change risk that might lead to different mitigative behaviours. Some scholars in this field argue that perceptions of risk are formed in the context of a range of social, cultural and political factors. Wynne (1992), for instance, demonstrates that conflict between experts and the lay public may result from competition or a clash between their respective cultures. Wynne shows that because scientists have been socialized to evaluate phenomena empirically and claim objectivity, they are not receptive to the contributions of local 'experts' who may lack traditional academic credentials. Local lay people, in turn, view scientists as agents of those in power, and do not trust their methods. As a result, conflicts arise that appear to be about knowledge, when the catalyst for the conflict is actually threatened identities (Wynne, 1992). As climate change researchers begin to learn the value of local knowledge, similar conflicts may arise between scientists who may be viewed as capitalizing on the recent explosion of interest in the climate change issue, and local individuals who want to preserve (for instance) agriculture in vulnerable areas. Although, as mentioned, weather patterns may not be indicative of broader climate patterns, local and traditional knowledge may provide valuable insights into the nature of varying perceptions of climate change risk, and varying responses. This knowledge, however, and the concerns of those who possess it, is often undervalued by expert-driven cultures and thus under-represented in policy.

Added to this rational or analytical way of interpreting risk is an intuitive or affective layer of response, which has been termed the 'experiential system' (Slovic et al., 2004). This more rapid, mostly unconscious, evaluation of risk is thought to operate in parallel with our more logical assessments of risk, and the two systems fundamentally guide and inform one another (Slovic et al., 2004). This role of affect in thinking and information processing has gained visibility in the risk community (Kahneman and Frederick, 2002; Slovic et al., 2002), and draws our attention to the ways in which rationality and emotion are inextricably linked. This complicated relationship may shed some light on varying responses to the risk of climate change (of which few of us have experience) and may help explain why, in cases such as this where consequences are new or unexpected, the 'affect heuristic' fails to enable us to be rational actors.

Psychological and socio-cultural models of risk perception and response point to the fact that varying responses to climate change might indeed be rational. Incorporating local and lay knowledge, addressing concerns of environmental injustice and social inequity, and formulating programmes that account for variation in social hierarchies and group integration might help to resolve part of the controversy that arises from different mitigative behaviour, and help to close the apparent gap between capacity and action in response to climate change.

Risk perception, whether defined through psychological or socio-cultural models, is not incorporated into the current definition of response capacity, but can clearly influence behaviour. A high perception of the risks associated with global climate change, for instance, might provide the foundation of interest in climate change adaptation or mitigation and knowledge of the benefits of adaptation or mitigation that is needed to effect behaviour change. Similarly, a community that perceives a high level of risk might also utilize the social forces that encourage and reinforce adaptive or mitigative behaviour.

5. Conclusions and future directions

This article has introduced the concept of response capacity, and traced its links to adaptive and mitigative capacity, and ultimately action or behaviour change in response to climate change. This complex and dynamic set of relationships is deeply embedded within the underlying development path, pointing to the need to consider integrated adaptive and mitigative responses. Risk perception has been presented, for illustrative purposes, as only one of many socio-cultural characteristics that may influence the relationship between capacity and action, and thus shape responses to climate change. It is necessary to further elaborate upon other factors that may also fundamentally alter human responses to this risk, in order to stimulate sufficient greenhouse gas reduction and adaptation strategies. For this, one must look to the literatures of institutional genesis and change, socio-technical systems, social movements, and collective behaviour change theory (to name but a few) to shed light on the underlying development paths which influence both capacity and action.

Similarly, from the point of view of policy, and moving more readily from capacity to action, the concept of response capacity and the socio-economic and technological development pathways such capacity is embedded within, suggest the need to consider carefully the socio-technical context within which climate policy responses must be undertaken. Actions inconsistent with development-path trajectories are likely to face greater hurdles in implementation and may, indeed, not be given serious consideration. Whether adaptive and mitigative measures and actions are likely to compete for resources or else reinforce each other will likewise depend, in part, on the nature of the development path within which they are expressed.

To the extent that climate change policies are increasingly framed in terms of sustainability goals, then the arguments presented in this article suggest that a crucial consideration must be the question of how it may be possible to make a transition from currently dominant development paths to sustainable ones. This, in turn, not only shifts the focus of concern somewhat from climate policy to sustainability policy (Swart et al., 2003; Robinson et al., 2006), but also suggests the importance of investigating and developing effective means by which perceived barriers can be overcome at the municipal, regional, national and international scales.

Note

1. This was a common focus throughout the First and Second Assessment Reports, but became especially prevalent in the reports of Working Groups II and III of the Second Assessment Report (IPCC, 1995a; 1995b).

References

Adger, W.N., Huq, S., Brown, K., Conway, D., Hulme, M., 2003, 'Adaptation to climate change in the developing world', *Progress in Development Studies* 3(3), 179–195.
Adger, W.N., Brooks, N., Kelly, M., Bentham, G., Agnew, M., Eriksen, S., 2004, *New Indicators of Vulnerability and Adaptive Capacity*, Technical Report 7, Tyndall Centre for Climate Change Research, Norwich, UK.
Adger, W.N., Agrawala, S., Mirza, M.M.Q., Conde, C., O'Brien, K., Puhlin, J., Pulwarty, R., Smit, B., Takahashi, K., 2007, 'Assessment of adaptation practices, options, constraints and capacity', *Climate Change 2007: Impacts, Adaptation and Vulnerability. Contribution of Working Group II to the Fourth Assessment Report of the Intergovernmental Panel on Climate Change*, M.L. Parry, O.F. Canziani, J.P. Palutikof, P.J. van der Linden, C.E. Hansen (eds), Cambridge University Press, Cambridge, UK, 717–743.
Banuri, T., Weyant, J., Akumu, G., Najam, A., Pinguielli Rosa, L., Rayner, S., Sachs, W., Sharma, R., Yohe, G., 2001, 'Setting the stage: climate change and sustainable development', in: B. Metz, O. Davidson, R. Swart, J. Pan (eds),

Climate Change 2001: Mitigation, Report of Working Group III, Intergovernmental Panel on Climate Change, Cambridge University Press, Cambridge, UK.

Beg, N., Morlot, J.C., Davidson, O., Afrane-Okesse, Y., Tyani, L., Denton, F., Sokona, Y., Thomas, J.P., La Rovere, E.L., Parikh, J.K., Parikh, K., Atiq Rahman, A., 2002, 'Linkages between climate change and sustainable development', *Climate Policy* 2(2), 129–144.

Berkes, F., Colding, J., Folke, C., 2000a, 'Rediscovery of traditional ecological knowledge as adaptive management', *Ecological Applications* 10(5), 1251–1262.

Berkes, F., Folke, C., Colding, J., 2000b, *Linking Social and Ecological Systems: Management Practices and Social Mechanisms for Building Resilience*, Cambridge University Press, Cambridge, UK.

Betsill, M., 2001, 'Mitigating climate change in US cities: opportunities and obstacles', *Local Environment* 6(4), 393–406.

Bizikova, L., Robinson, J., Cohen, S., 2007, 'Linking climate change and sustainable development at the local level', *Climate Policy* 7(4), 271–277.

Brooks, N., Adger, W.N., Kelly, P.M., 2005, 'The determinants of vulnerability and adaptive capacity at the national level and the implications for adaptation', *Global Environmental Change* 15, 151–163.

Bullard, R., 1994, 'Decision making', *Environment* 36(4), 11–20, 39–44.

CIA, 2004, *CIA World Factbook*, Central Intelligence Agency [available at https://www.cia.gov/library/publications/the-world-factbook/docs/gallery.html].

Cohen, S., Demeritt, D., Robinson, J., Rothman, D., 1998, 'Climate change and sustainable development: towards dialogue', *Global Environmental Change* 8(4), 341–371.

Dang, H.H., Michaelowa, A., Tuan, D.D., 2003, 'Synergy of adaptation and mitigation strategies in the context of sustainable development: the case of Vietnam', *Climate Policy* 3(S1), S81–S96.

Dietz, T., Stern, P.C., Guagnano, G., 1998, 'Social structure and social psychological bases of environmental concern', *Environment and Behaviour* 30, 450–471.

Folke, C., Carpenter, S., Elmqvist, T., Gunderson, L., Holling, C., Walker, B., 2002, 'Resilience and sustainable development: building adaptive capacity in a world of transformations', *Ambio* 31(5), 437–440.

Grothmann, T., Patt, A., 2005, 'Adaptive capacity and human cognition: the process of individual adaptation to climate change', *Global Environment Change* 15(3), 199–213.

Haddad, B., 2005, 'Ranking the adaptive capacity of nations to climate change when socio-political goals are explicit', *Global Environmental Change* 15, 165–176.

Hawley, A.H., 1986, *Human Ecology: A Theoretical Essay*, University of Chicago Press, Chicago.

Holling, C.S., 1978, *Adaptive Environmental Assessment and Management*, Wiley, New York.

Holling, C.S., 1986, 'The resilience of terrestrial ecosystems: local surprise and global change', in: W. Clark, R. Munn (eds), *Sustainable Development of the Biosphere*, Cambridge University Press, Cambridge, UK.

IPCC, 1995a, *Climate Change 1995: Impacts, Adaptations and Mitigation of Climate Change: Scientific-Technical Analyses. Contribution of Working Group II to the Second Assessment of the Intergovernmental Panel on Climate Change (IPCC)*, R.T. Watson, M.C. Zinyowera, R.H. Moss (eds), Cambridge University Press, Cambridge, UK and New York.

IPCC, 1995b, *Climate Change 1995: Economic and Social Dimensions of Climate Change. Contribution of Working Group III to the Second Assessment of the Intergovernmental Panel on Climate Change*, J.P. Bruce, H. Lee, E.F. Haites (eds), Cambridge University Press, Cambridge, UK and New York.

IPCC, 2001a, *Climate Change 2001: Impacts, Adaptation and Vulnerability. Contribution of Working Group II to the Third Assessment Report of the Intergovernmental Panel on Climate Change*, J.J. McCarthy, O.F. Canziani, N.A. Leary, D.J. Dokken, K.S. White (eds), Cambridge University Press, Cambridge, UK and New York.

IPCC, 2001b, *Climate Change 2001: Mitigation. Contribution of Working Group III to the Third Assessment Report of the Intergovernmental Panel on Climate Change (IPCC)*, B. Metz, O. Davidson, R. Swart, J. Pan (eds), Cambridge University Press, Cambridge, UK and New York.

Irwin, A., 1995, *Citizen Science*, Routledge, New York.

Irwin, A., Wynne, B., 1996, *Misunderstanding Science? The Public Reconstruction of Science*, Cambridge University Press, Cambridge, UK.

Jasanoff, S., Wynne, B., 1998, 'Science and Decisionmaking', in: S. Rayner, E. Malone (eds), *Human Choice and Climate Change, Vol. 1: The Societal Framework*, Batelle Press, Columbus, OH.

Jones, R.N., Dettmann, P., Park, G., Rogers, M., White, T., 2007, 'The relationship between adaptation and mitigation in managing climate risks: a regional response from North Central Victoria, Australia', *Mitigation and Adaptation Strategies for Global Change* 12, 685–712.

Kahneman, D., Frederick, S., 2002, 'Representativeness revisited: attribute substitution in intuitive judgement', in: T. Gilovich, D. Griffin, D. Kahneman (eds), *Heuristics and Biases: The Psychology of Intuitive Judgment*, Cambridge University Press, New York, 49–81.

Kempton, W., 1997, 'How the public views climate change', *Environment* 39(9), 13–21.

Klein, R.J.T., Huq, S., Denton, F., Downing, T.E., Richels, R.G., Robinson, J.B., Toth, F.L., 2007: 'Inter-relationships between adaptation and mitigation', *Climate Change 2007: Impacts, Adaptation and Vulnerability. Contribution of Working Group II to the Fourth Assessment Report of the Intergovernmental Panel on Climate Change*. M.L. Parry, O.F. Canziani, J.P. Palutikof, P.J. van der Linden, C.E. Hanson (eds), Cambridge University Press, Cambridge, UK, 745–777.

Kollmuss, A., Agyeman, J., 2002, 'Mind the gap: why do people act environmentally, and what are the barriers to pro-environmental behavior?', *Environmental Education Research* 8(3), 239–260.

Lowe, T., Brown, K., Dessai, S., de França Doria, M., Haynes, K., Vincent, K., 2006, 'Does tomorrow ever come? Disaster narrative and public perceptions of climate change', *Public Understanding of Science* 15, 435–457.

Moss, R., Brenkert, A.L., Malone, E.L., 2001, *Vulnerability to Climate Change: A Quantitative Approach*, Pacific Northwest National Laboratory.

Robinson, J., Bradley, M., Busby, P., Connor, D., Murray, A., Sampson, B., Soper, W., 2006, 'Climate change and sustainable development: realizing the opportunity', *Ambio* 35(1), 2–8.

Sagar, A.D., 2000, 'Capacity development for the environment: a view for the South, a view for the North', *Annual Review of Energy and the Environment* 25(1), 377–439.

Sathaye, J.A., Najam, A., Cocklin, C., Heller, T., Lecocq, F., Llanes-Regueiro, J., Pan, J., Petschel-Held, G., Rayner, S., Robinson, J., Schaeffer, R., Sokona, Y., Swart, R., Winkler, H., 2007, 'Sustainable Development and Mitigation', in *Climate Change 2007: Mitigation. Contribution of Working Group III to the Fourth Assessment Report of the Intergovernmental Panel on Climate Change*, B. Metz, O.R. Davidson, P.R. Bosch, R. Dave, L.A. Meyer (eds), Cambridge University Press, Cambridge, UK and New York.

Satterfield, T., Mertz, C., Slovic, P., 2004, 'Discrimination, vulnerability, and justice in the face of risk', *Risk Analysis* 24(1), 115–129.

Slovic, P., 1992, 'Perceptions of risk: reflections on the psychometric paradigm', in: *Social Theories of Risk*, Praeger, Westport, CT.

Slovic, P., Finucane, M.L., Peters, E., MacGregor, D.G., 2002, 'The affect heuristic', in: T. Gilovich, D. Griffin, D. Kahneman (eds), *Heuristics and Biases: The Psychology of Intuitive Judgement*, Cambridge University Press, New York, 397–420.

Slovic, P., Finucane, M.L., Peters, E., MacGregor, D.G., 2004, 'Risk as analysis and risk as feelings: some thoughts about affect, reason, risk, and rationality', *Risk Analysis* 24(2), 311–322.

Smit, B., Pilifosova, O., Burton, I., Challenger, B., Huq, S., Klein, R., Yohe, G., 2001, 'Adaptation to climate change in the context of sustainable development and equity', in: J. McCarthy, O. Canziani, N. Leary, D. Dokken, K. White (eds), *Climate Change 2001: Impacts, Adaptation and Vulnerability*, Cambridge University Press, Cambridge, UK.

Stern, P.C., 2000, 'Toward a coherent theory of environmentally significant behavior', *Journal of Social Issues* 56(3), 407–424.

Swart, R., Robinson, J., Cohen, S., 2003, 'Climate change and sustainable development: expanding the options', *Climate Policy* 3(S1), S19–S40.

Tompkins, E., Adger, W.N., 2005, 'Defining response capacity to enhance climate change policy', *Environmental Sciences and Policy* 8, 562–571.

UNFCCC, 2005, *Key GHG Data*, UNFCCC.

Wilbanks, T., Kates, R.W., 1999, 'Global change in local places: how scale matters', *Climatic Change* 43, 601–628.

Wilbanks, T., Sathaye, J., 2007, 'Integrating mitigation and adaptation as responses to climate change', *Mitigation and Adaptation Strategies for Global Change* 12, 957–962.

Wilbanks, T., Leiby, P., Perlack, R.D., Ensminger, J.T., Wright, S.B., 2007, 'Toward an integrated analysis of mitigation and adaptation: some preliminary findings', *Mitigation and Adaptation Strategies for Global Change* 12, 713–725.

Winkler, H., Baumert, K., Blanchard, O., Burch, S., Robinson, J., 2007, 'What factors influence mitigative capacity?', *Energy Policy* 35(1), 692–703.

Wynne, B., 1992, 'Misunderstood misunderstanding: social identities and public uptake of science', *Public Understanding of Science* 1(3), 281–304.

Yohe, G.W., 2001, 'Mitigative capacity: the mirror image of adaptive capacity on the emissions side', *Climatic Change* 49(3), 247–262.

Yohe, G., Strzepek, K., 2007, 'Adaptation and mitigation as complementary tools for reducing the risk of climate impacts', *Mitigation and Adaptation Strategies for Global Change* 12, 727–739.

■ synthesis article

Understanding and managing the complexity of urban systems under climate change

MATTHIAS RUTH[1,2,3]*, DANA COELHO[1]

[1] Center for Integrative Environmental Research, Division of Research, University of Maryland, Van Munching Hall, Suite 2202, College Park, MD 20742, USA

[2] Environmental Policy Program, School of Public Policy, University of Maryland, Van Munching Hall, Suite 2202, College Park, MD 20742, USA

[3] Engineering and Public Policy, A. James Clark School of Engineering and School of Public Policy, University of Maryland, Van Munching Hall, Suite 2202, College Park, MD 20742, USA

Recent case studies for individual locations and on individual urban challenges reveal the growing complexity of managing interrelations among population, infrastructure and institutions. Climate change is increasing the pressures on many urban systems and adding to this complexity. Many of the case studies investigating urban dynamics in the light of climate change have chosen narrow, sector-specific approaches. Few projects have built on insights from complexity theory and related bodies of knowledge which are more consistent with the perspective that urban infrastructure systems are tightly coupled with one another and must respond to often subtle, long-term changes of technological, social and environmental conditions. Drawing on that knowledge, and building on insights from previous case studies, this article explores the potential roles of complexity theory in guiding investment and policy decisions in the urban context. Policy and management that are consistent with insights from complexity theory will need to anticipate a wide array of potential trajectories for urban dynamics, identify and implement strategies that are robust under a range of potential developments, continuously innovate the policy-making and management institutions, and intensify the exchange of knowledge between science and society.

Keywords: adaptation; adaptive management; climate change; cities; complex systems; environmental impact; infrastructure; public policy; urban resilience

Des études de cas récentes appliquées à des régions spécifiques et des défis urbains spécifiques révèlent une complexité croissante dans la gestion des liens entre population, infrastructure et cadre institutionnel. Le changement climatique accroît la pression sur de nombreux systèmes urbains, augmentant ainsi leur complexité existante. Un grand nombre de ces études de cas examinant les dynamiques urbaines dans le cadre du changement climatique est fondé sur des approches sectorielles étroites.

Peu de projets ont intégré les connaissances issues des théories de la complexité et autres disciplines liées, celles-ci étant plus en accord avec l'idée que les systèmes d'infrastructure urbaine sont intimement liés entre eux et doivent souvent s'adapter à des changements subtils, et de long terme, qu'ils soient d'ordre technologique, social ou environnemental. A partir de ces connaissances et de résultats d'études de cas antérieures, cet article explore les rôles potentiels de la théorie de la complexité dans la prise de décision politique ou financière dans le contexte urbain. Une politique et une gestion en phase avec les connaissances issues de la théorie de la complexité devra anticiper une multitude de trajectoires potentielles en dynamique urbaine, identifier et mettre en place des stratégies robustes dans divers scenarios potentiels, innover de manière continue les institutions de politique et de gestion, et intensifier les échanges des connaissances entre science et société.

Mots clés: adaptation; changement du climat; cites; gestion adaptive; impact environnemental; infrastructure; politiques publiques; résilience urbaine; systèmes complexes

■ *Corresponding author. E-mail*: mruth1@umd.edu

1. Introduction

As the number of people and the volume and intensity of economic activities in cities are growing worldwide, the influence of cities on the local and global environment is increasing. The repercussions of this environmental change, in turn, are felt by the inhabitants of cities and their hinterlands, as well as by the economic sectors that sustain livelihoods.

Climate change, with its impacts on infrastructures and the socioeconomic fabric of cities, poses qualitatively new challenges for analysis and decision-making in the urban context. With their concentration of economic activity, urban areas contribute significantly to the emissions of greenhouse gases. As they begin to recognize their role as a contributor to global climate change, cities – through intricate changes in behaviours and the built environment – are attempting to cut emissions. But since past emissions will continue to influence climate for decades to come, cities must also begin to adapt to the impacts of climate change on both the infrastructures that influence urban living as well as broader climate-induced regional, national and global environmental and socioeconomic trends.

Traditional urban analysis has focused on the drivers behind urban change and discrete impacts on people, the economy, and the environment (e.g. Robson, 1969; Dear and Dishman, 2002). Although urban systems analysis is often rich in empirical detail or theoretical conceptualizations dealing with both the temporal and spatial dimensions of urban change (e.g. Black and Henderson, 1999; Fujita et al., 1999; Brenner, 2000), the interconnection among the various drivers and repercussions – social, economic and environmental – has frequently been acknowledged but has rarely become, in its own right, the object of analysis. Where the focus truly has been on the complexity of urban change, the products were often either computer-based exercises or conceptual frameworks. Most popular among the former are simulation games, such as SimCity™ (EAI, 2005), which concentrate on the evolution of a hypothetical or stylized urban system. In such games, a single player interferes in a system's dynamics through choice variables and learns to appreciate the complexity and uncertainty inherent in system intervention.

Examples of systematic, theory-based conceptualizations of urban change include work by Peter Nijkamp and colleagues (e.g. Nijkamp and Reggiani, 1992; Camagni et al., 1998), Jan Rotmans (1994, 2006), Michael Batty (2005), Patsy Healey (2007) and a large number of others, many of whom have begun to view urban dynamics through the lens of modern complexity theory. Some of the recent research in this area illustrates a merger between urban simulation and complex systems analysis, by explicitly basing computer simulations of urban dynamics on, and interpreting outcomes of urban dynamics from the perspective of, complexity theory. We will briefly discuss some of these studies in more detail below.

More recently, a new flavour of urban analysis has developed, one that is pragmatic in nature and that combines, among other approaches, theoretical, empirical, simulation-based and stakeholder-guided assessments. The pragmatic aspect of the research lies in the identification and study of issues relevant to decision-makers, and in efforts to make findings relevant to the decision-making process. Much of that work has been spawned by the debate about regional impacts of, and adaptations to, climate change (Ruth, 2006a). While promising in many regards, several challenges remain for that work to be academically rigorous and, at the same time, relevant for investment and policy-making. The discussion below addresses the state of the art, critically summarizes the promises that integrated analysis holds for advancing knowledge and improving decision-making in the urban context, and highlights the lingering challenges.

With the aim of contributing to the advancement of urban systems analysis for the management of urban systems, this article first briefly reviews traditional urban assessments via biophysical approaches as well as socioeconomic, institutional and political approaches. The two sets of approaches provide complementary perspectives on complex urban change processes. The subsequent section then discusses drivers behind urban change. Here we concentrate on general urbanization trends, the role and state of infrastructures and institutions that manage the urban system, changes in urban metabolism, and urban environmental quality. The discussion of previous approaches and recognition of key attributes of the drivers behind urban change raises issues germane to the study of complex systems, which we address in Section 4. Here, we distinguish between descriptive or simulation-oriented studies and efforts to use the insights from complexity theory to shape the way in which urban systems analysis is carried out in interaction with stakeholders. We close with a brief summary and conclusions.

2. Urban regional assessments

Recognition of the interrelationships between environmental, economic and social changes in the urban context has spawned research programmes to improve knowledge about their respective roles and to use that knowledge as an input into policy and investment decision-making. Two related strands of research are discussed here. The first concentrates on monitoring and understanding biophysical processes and associated technological change, the second more readily addresses the interdependencies of environmental, socioeconomic and institutional change in cities.

2.1. Environmental change in cities

Among the first efforts to advance understanding of urban environmental processes from a basic science perspective in the USA are the Long Term Ecological Research (LTER) programmes established by the US National Science Foundation. The LTER programmes, established in 1980, support interdisciplinary research at 26 sites across the USA. Research projects investigate ecological processes – and, in the case of the two urban LTER sites (Central Arizona–Phoenix and Baltimore, Maryland), social–ecological interactions – over large temporal and spatial scales (NSF, 1997, 2000).

Research at the two urban LTER sites recognizes the fundamental importance of humans in urban landscapes and seeks to place humans within the context of larger ecosystems. Studies at the urban LTER sites are being carried out in geographically, hydrologically, socially and economically distinct places. Phoenix is a relatively young city on the rise but constrained, in part, by significant water stress and traffic congestion. Baltimore, on the other hand, suffers degraded infrastructure, crime, population decline and water pollution.

Non-governmental organizations (NGOs) have also promoted awareness and responses to climate change at the urban level, such as the International Council of Local Environmental Initiatives (ICLEI) Climate Protection Campaign. Similar and related (applied) research programmes are being promoted in Europe, such as through the BEQUEST (Building Environmental Quality Evaluation for Sustainability through Time) Network (Curwell and Deakin, 2002), the EU Fifth Framework Programme on the 'Cities of Tomorrow' (European Commission, 2006) and the International Human Dimensions Programme on Global Environmental Change (IHDP) on 'Cities and Industrial Transformation' (IHDP, 2001).

2.2. Integrated urban assessment of global change impacts

Significantly younger than the LTER sites, and less formally connected, are a host of current urban assessment projects that were spawned by the recognition that global environmental change

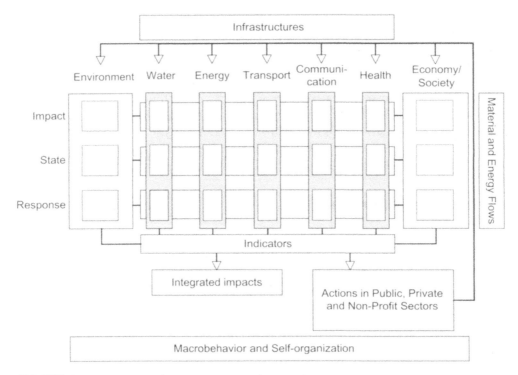

FIGURE 1 Integrated urban impact assessment framework.

influences urban dynamics. These projects have paid special attention to the influences of climatic change on the adequacy and reliability of urban infrastructures, and associated changes in urban environmental quality and quality of life. In many instances, the underlying conceptual framework for analysis is some variant of the 'drivers–pressure–state–impacts–response' (DPSIR) approach proposed by the OECD (1993) and widely used by the European Environment Agency (1998) and other institutions. In its basic form, it distinguishes environmental, economic and social components of the (urban) system, sometimes with a refined representation of individual infrastructure elements and their relationship to each other and to the overarching socioeconomic and environmental system as shown in Figure 1. Broad socioeconomic and global climatic conditions, that together bracket the development of infrastructures, can be captured in scenarios. Within this context, the state of a particular infrastructure is influenced and responds, in part, to direct impacts, and in part to changes elsewhere in the larger system.

Integrated urban assessments, for each selected system element, describe its state, identify impacts on the respective element, and determine the responses of system elements to impacts. For example, water treatment infrastructure may be characterized by treatment capacities and capacity utilization. Impacts on those state variables may come from changes in population, economic activity, technology, or rainfall and runoff. Responses may be in the form of system failure, retrofits, upgrades, or changes in technology or demand elsewhere in the larger system. In many instances, changes in one element of the system (e.g. water treatment) may trigger changes elsewhere (e.g. energy supply for water treatment), thus creating ripple effects often with time-lagged and non-linear relationships to the original stimulus for change.

Indicators for element-specific and integrated (system-wide) impacts are quantified to inform investment and policy choices, which in turn feed back as new impacts to influence system states.

System changes are related (or, at least in principle, relatable) to the metabolism and overall macrobehaviours and emergent properties of the city. The latter are the subject of the next section of this article.

Examples of more narrow assessments of global change impacts on cities – without explicitly accounting for material and energy flows and without explicit efforts to provide a complex systems perspective to the emergent behaviours – are presented in Table 1. This table suggests that, more recently, urban integrated assessments have generally become more ambitious with respect to the number of infrastructure systems and interactions they analyse, the diversity and roles of stakeholders, and the diversity and sophistication of methods and tools used to carry out the research. Still somewhat relegated to the sidelines are the actual social dynamics that accompany urban impacts and adaptations to climate change. This is largely true for the urban LTER projects discussed above.

Examples of larger-scale analyses that cover a mix of rural and urban areas and explicitly deal with underlying social issues include the work by Holman et al. (2005a, 2005b) for East Anglia and north-west England. However, there, partly to be able to deal with a larger area and to include social dynamics, the resolution with respect to individual system components (infrastructures, economic sectors, etc.) remains relatively low, compared with the narrower, urban-region-focused studies presented in Table 1.

Despite the advances in modelling and analysis of complex urban dynamics brought about by all of these studies, the field of integrated urban impact assessment is young and remains disconnected from, for example, basic science approaches as illustrated in the urban LTER projects and similar efforts around the world. At the same time, insights from complexity theory have only implicitly guided the design of these studies and the interpretation of results.

The following section addresses drivers and impacts of urban change. Section 4 then follows with specific issues germane to the study of complex systems and the application of insights from complex systems theory to urban analysis and modelling.

3. Drivers and impacts of urban change

3.1. Urbanization trends

Urbanization is globally on the rise, though significant regional differences in both the patterns and rates of urbanization exist. The world has seen a 15-fold increase in urban populations since the beginning of the 20th century, with total urban-dwellers numbering close to 3 billion in 2000, roughly half of the global population. These 3 billion people occupy only 2.8% of the total land area of the earth, but exert locally and globally significant influence on ecosystems and the well-being of human populations within and outside of their borders. In 2000, as measured by the United Nations (UN) Global Rural–Urban Mapping Project (GRUMP), approximately 37% of the populations in Africa and Asia were urban (UNDP, 2003). The number is closer to 75% in Latin America and the Caribbean, North America, Europe and Oceania (McGranahan and Marcotullio, 2006). As can be seen in Table 2, both total population and urban population at all levels of development are increasing, though at a decreasing rate. Consistently, wealthier and more developed nations are characterized by greater levels of urbanization, though the majority of urban *growth* is occurring in less developed nations. Indeed, urbanization in the least developed places is as much as four times that in the most developed nations.

A great deal of attention has recently been given to mega-cities (10 million or more people), but this focus is somewhat inflated; about half of the world's urban population lives in cities of less than 500,000 people, and the majority of urban growth is occurring in medium-sized cities

TABLE 1 Integrated assessments of climate impacts and adaptation in urban areas

	Bloomfield et al. (1999)	Koteen et al. (2001)	Rosenzweig et al. (2000)	Kirshen et al. (2004)	Hoo and Sumitani (2005)	Jollands et al. (2005, 2006)	Lange and Garrelts (2006)
Location	Greater Los Angeles, CA, USA	New York, USA	Metropolitan New York, USA	Metropolitan Boston, MA, USA	Metropolitan Seattle, WA, USA	Hamilton and Wellington NZ	Hamburg and Bremen, Germany
Coverage:							
Water supply	X	X	X	X		X	X
Water quality				X		X	X
Water demand				X		X	X
Sea-level rise	X		X	X	X		X
Transportation				X	X	X	X
Communication							X
Energy			X	X		X	
Public health							
Vector-borne diseases							
Food-borne diseases	X						
Temperature-related mortality							
Temperature-related morbidity	X	X		X		X	
Air-quality related mortality			X			X	
Air-quality related morbidity			X			X	
Other	X	X	X			X	X
Ecosystems							
Wetlands							
Other (wildfires)	X		X				
Urban forests (trees & vegetation)		X			X		
Air quality		X				X	

Extent of:							
Quantitative analysis	Low	Medium	Medium	High	Low	High	Medium
Computer-based modelling	None	Low	Low	High	None	Medium	None
Scenario analysis	None	None	Medium	High	Medium	Medium	Medium
Explicit risk analysis	None	None	None	None	None	Medium	High
Involvement of:							
Local planning agencies	None	None	High	High	High	High	High
Local government agencies	None	None	High	High	High	High	High
Private industry	None	None	None	Low	None	None	Low
Non-profits	None	None	Low	High	None	None	Medium
Citizens	None	None	None	Medium	None	None	Low
Identification of:							
Adaptation options	X	X	X	X	X	X	X
Adaptation cost			X	X		X	
Extent of integration across systems	None	None	Low	Medium	Low	High	Low

TABLE 2 Total and urban population trends by level of development and income, 1975–2015

	1975		2001		1975–2001		2015		2001–2015	
	Total (million)	Urban (%)	Total (million)	Urban (%)	Total (% Δ)	Urban (% Δ)	Total (million)	Urban (%)	Total (% Δ)	Urban (% Δ)
High HDI	972.3	71.7	1,193.9	78.3	0.8	9.2%	1,282.0	81.5	0.5	4.1%
Medium HDI	2,678.4	28.1	4,116.2	41.6	1.7	48.0%	4,759.1	49.4	1.0	18.8%
Low HDI	354.5	19.1	737.5	31.6	2.8	65.5%	1,021.6	39.7	2.3	25.6%
High income	782.0	73.8	935.9	79.4	0.7	7.6%	997.7	82.6	0.5	4.0%
Middle income	1,847.5	35.0	2,694.8	51.6	1.5	47.4%	3,027.9	60.7	0.8	17.6%
Low income	1,437.1	22.1	2,515.0	31.5	2.2	42.5%	3,169.0	38.1	1.7	21.0%
World	4,068.1	37.9	6,148.1	47.7	1.6	25.9%	7,197.2	53.7	1.1	12.6%

Source: UNDP (2003).

(McGranahan and Marcotullio, 2006). In fact, some of the world's largest cities have experienced slowed growth rates in recent decades. This is not to diminish the fact that the average size of the world's 100 largest cities has increased from 200,000 in 1800 to 5 million in 1990 (Cohen, 2004). This trend is anticipated to continue. In efforts to keep up with and sometimes stimulate urban growth, transportation and communication networks – two of a city's most extensive infrastructure systems – are expanding.

The age composition within nations and within cities is also changing, with populations aging across the board. That demographic change has far-reaching implications for migration to and from cities, demand for urban infrastructure, urban material and energy use, environmental quality, and quality of life. The most pronounced change is seen in middle-income and medium human development nations, where UN projections for the period between 2001 and 2015 are for an almost 17% decrease in the percentage of the population under the age of 15, and a more than 25% increase in the percentage of the population over the age of 65. Decreases in youth populations of 12 and 6% are anticipated in high and low human development nations, respectively. Increases of 23 and 7% in the elderly population are anticipated in these nations.

In addition to purely demographic changes are a suite of environmental conditions that are influencing and being affected by urbanization. Most cities are located in, and are growing in, coastal zones, in part because of the importance of access to natural resources and transportation networks in an increasingly globalizing world. Population densities in coastal areas are approximately 45% greater than the global average (McGranahan and Marcotullio, 2006). For example, 32% of Sri Lanka's total population, 65% of the urban population, 90% of industrial units, and 80% of all tourist infrastructure are found in coastal zones (UNEP, 2001c). Unprecedented stress to coastal ecosystems, as well as unprecedented vulnerabilities of settlements and populations, is resulting from this confluence of factors.

3.2. Urban infrastructures and institutions

3.2.1. Infrastructure trends

An adequate supply of infrastructure systems and services, such as water, sanitation, power, communication and transportation, allows a city to grow and prosper. In some regions, particularly in Africa and Asia, very basic deficiencies characterize urban systems of all sizes. According to some estimates, as much as 50% of the urban population in Africa and Asia may be living without 'adequate' provision of water and sanitary services. In many of these areas, single points of service (e.g. water pumps or latrines) are shared by dozens or hundreds of individuals, significantly limiting sufficient access and safety. Similarly, solid waste disposal, wastewater treatment, and transportation networks are frequently insufficient and poorly maintained (UNEP, 2001b, 2001c).

However, the challenges of inadequate or declining infrastructures are not confined to the developing world. In some developed nations, particularly Australia, public spending on infrastructure has decreased over the last few decades. Private investment in the provision of electricity and water has increased, but distribution suffers from decentralized services, and concerns abound over the ability of profit-seeking firms to equitably provide public services such as water and transportation (Newton, 2001). This concern is pervasive not only in Australia, but in other nations as well (World Bank, 2006). In the USA, infrastructure systems have regularly received 'poor' or 'failing' grades in report cards issued by the American Society of Civil Engineers (ASCE, 2005). ASCE evaluates infrastructure systems based on condition and performance, as well as capacity and funding with respect to need. Based on their analysis, about US$1.6 trillion needs to be spent on recommended infrastructure improvements over the coming 5 years.

3.2.2. Institutional management

It is the role of institutions such as government and planning agencies, markets, and non-government organizations to anticipate and assess the adequacy of existing infrastructure and the desirability of new infrastructure, to facilitate decision-making, and to oversee implementation, operation, maintenance and decommissioning of infrastructure systems. This is particularly crucial in cities, given the close spatial and functional relationships among the various social, economic and environmental processes. Challenges in fulfilling that mission are often related to inabilities to secure adequate funds, inequitable access, the lumpiness and irreversibility of infrastructure investments, and the roles of risk, uncertainty and surprise in investment decision-making. Each challenge is discussed briefly here, before we turn to the ramifications of urbanization for material and energy use, environmental quality, and quality of life.

INFRASTRUCTURE INVESTMENT

Typically, large-scale infrastructure investments are undertaken by government to provide public goods. Examples include the building of dams, wastewater collection and treatment systems, energy supply systems, ports, and roads (see, e.g., Guy, 1996). However, investment by private enterprises in infrastructure systems should not be overlooked. Notable examples include investments in communication and data storage capacity that made possible the explosion in information exchange and Internet commerce (Graham and Marvin, 1996; Davison et al., 2000). While public investments are typically funded with long-term bonds or loans and with the goal of providing public goods, private infrastructure investments are usually made with much shorter time periods in mind, and with greater attention towards payoffs to the investing parties.

Increasingly, public–private partnerships are used to leverage access to capital with clear profitability goals in mind, while at the same time creating synergistic effects among infrastructure investments, regional competitiveness, and larger-scale socioeconomic development. For example, funding for transportation networks or wastewater treatment may come in part from private enterprises who may, in return, receive revenues from user fees. Private investment in electricity and telecommunications infrastructure in Latin America has increased access to services; however, overall public investment in infrastructure fell from 3% of GDP in 1980 to less than 1% in 2001 (World Bank, 2006). Local authorities may help support the development of eco-industrial parks so that a range of diverse businesses can co-locate in close proximity to one another in order to close material cycles, reduce the cost of material inputs and minimize effluents, while at the same time offering centralized employment opportunities and improved environmental quality. The reduction in investment risk is spread across different parties, allowing for longer planning horizons than would be chosen by private enterprises under normal circumstances.

However, under any model – purely public, purely private, or public–private partnerships – few provisions are typically made to deal with the cost associated with decommissioning infrastructure at the end of its useful life or the cost of retrofitting after expiration of bonds or loans. As a result, the time-delayed burden to deal with the legacy of obsolete infrastructure is often placed on future generations, which contributes to the complexity of urban dynamics and adds challenges to future decision-making.

EQUITABLE ACCESS TO INFRASTRUCTURE SYSTEMS AND SERVICES

Criteria for equality and fairness must include the needs of current and future businesses and households at different locations in the economic landscape. While their needs for infrastructure services will influence the choice of location and type of infrastructure systems, the reverse holds as well – once put in place, infrastructure will affect the economic performance of businesses and income of households, as well as their need for infrastructure services. Access to infrastructure, in turn, determines access to resources (natural and human-made) and thus affects quality of life.

As a consequence, equality and fairness in space are closely related to equality and fairness through time and across different parts of the socioeconomic system (small and large producers, households from different income groups, etc.). These interrelationships are particularly pronounced in the development of urban relative to rural infrastructure. With urbanization increasing across the globe, the danger exists that infrastructure development will be concentrated in urban areas at the expense of the surrounding areas, which will miss out on investments.

The international community recognizes differential mobility, access to education, provision of clean water and sanitary sewer service, life expectancy, and exposure to disease between urban and rural areas, particularly to the extent that greater poverty is associated with rural areas (World Bank, 2006). For example, enlarged transportation networks entail problems that need to be dealt with, including those caused by the drainage of water from impervious surfaces, handling construction waste and managing larger traffic volumes. However, while rural poverty may, in absolute terms, be larger than that in cities, relative poverty suffered in cities – and in slums particularly – may be more devastating, because the urban poor are often more vulnerable to economic and political shifts and are more aware of their own poverty.

The presence or enlargement of one type of infrastructure system begets investments in another. Increased economic activity in cities and suburbs attracts companies and consumers alike to urban areas. Several consequences may be felt. Enlarging the urban–rural divide, with growing income differentials, may reduce the sustainability of rural life – undermining cultural and socioeconomic integrity. Conversely, high concentrations of people and economic activities may result in diseconomies of agglomeration, such as congestion, social friction, and consequently an unsustainable urban system.

The rate of change in urban densities themselves can make it virtually impossible for planners and investors to take a long view on infrastructure investment – current efforts to provide infrastructure may be inadequate to keep up with current growth in population and economic activity, let alone future needs or long-term environmental concerns. Those problems are exacerbated by the fact that the very activity of creating new infrastructure – both *hard* structures, such as bridges and sewerage systems, as well as the *soft* structures of institutions – disrupts the performance of already existing systems. For example, expanding or building a new transportation route will almost certainly affect the accessibility and operation of existing routes. Creating new bureaucracies inevitably raises, at least in the interim, information and transaction costs. But there is also the possibility for infrastructure change to leapfrog, as the example of wireless telecommunication technology in many transition economies shows – its development skipping the intermediate stages observed in already developed nations.

DEALING WITH INDIVISIBILITIES, COMPLEMENTARITIES AND IRREVERSIBILITIES IN INVESTMENT

Infrastructure systems, such as water supply, flood control, and transportation networks are typically large and often function as a whole or not at all. A break in a water main, dyke or bridge can render the respective system incapable of providing a service. Investment in redundancy is key to being prepared for disruptions, such as during construction or an emergency. For example, having well-developed private transportation, bus and rail systems in place can help to cut down on traffic jams in case one of the three is disrupted. Investing in redundancy, however, is costly. Similarly, ensuring adequate and reliable performance of one kind of infrastructure system often requires coordination with other systems. The smooth operation of highways, for example, may require the development of drainage and flood management systems. Not only are there opportunity costs to sinking large investments in complementary infrastructure systems, but such investments can cause irreversible environmental degradation – in addition to that caused by putting the primary system in place. Developing complementary infrastructure systems can also lead to technology lock-in (Arthur, 1989), and the associated phenomenon of carbon lock-in (Unruh, 2000). With few exceptions, urban transport systems around the world are directly or indirectly fossil-fuel based. The ease and reliability of movement that they guarantee has spawned suburbanization in much of the Western hemisphere, and has encouraged an increase in private car ownership, as well as the use of long-distance commuter buses and railways. With the enlarged role of these systems in modern day-to-day life, institutions have developed to manage these systems and to meet the needs of their constituents, and as a result have further locked in the existing infrastructure. As a consequence, institutional development in the past has often added to the inertia that makes adaptive management of infrastructure systems difficult in the light of changing environmental conditions or technologies (Unruh, 2002).

RISK, UNCERTAINTY AND SURPRISE IN THE PLANNING AND MANAGEMENT OF INFRASTRUCTURE SYSTEMS

Since infrastructure systems typically have long life spans, their presence reflects the knowledge and perceptions that decision-makers have about the physical, biological and economic environment, as well as their expectations for the future. Capacity and design criteria for infrastructure systems are typically based on historic observations and extrapolations into the future. Planners ask themselves: 'What will be the size and income of the population over the next 20 years?' 'What will be the rate of car ownership and travel demand?' 'What are likely changes in land use, industrial and residential location?' 'How rapidly will relative employment and output shift among sectors of the economy?' Answers to such questions are found on the basis of economic and planning models, most of which base their projections on an analysis of historical data. Safety margins are introduced into the projections to deal with risk and uncertainty.

Yet, since planners and decision-makers deal with socioeconomic systems that co-evolve in close relationship with other socioeconomic systems and their environment, there is ample room for surprises to occur and for projections to fail. For example, few investments in sea and airports, tunnels and roadways reflect the impacts that climate change may have on sea-level rise or increased adverse weather conditions, and therefore a need for better drainage and flood management. Current investments in transport infrastructure may also be misplaced if telecommuting and Internet commerce gain importance and lead to either a reduction in transport demand or increased (long-distance) transport of goods, services and people (Urri, 2000; Golob and Regan, 2001).

The size of capital requirements, long lifetimes, pivotal role in socioeconomic development, and environmental impacts of infrastructure require institutions to take the long view. At times of rapid change in population size, economic activity or technology, traditional methods of forecasting future demands for infrastructure systems and services on the basis of past trends is likely to be inadequate. By the same token, a host of large-scale, long-term drivers such as climate change require that current design criteria are revisited, and that existing and new infrastructure is (re-)built to withstand, for example, greater wind speeds, heavier snow and ice loads, higher surface temperatures, increased drought and precipitation, or elevated sea levels. As infrastructures adjust, volumes and patterns of material and energy use in urban areas (and their surroundings) change.

3.3. Changes in urban metabolism

Urban metabolism can be understood as the total flow of materials, energy and information into and out of an urban system (akin to the body's circulatory system) in order to generate goods and services (physical output) as well as increases in human well-being (non-material or social output) (Newcombe et al., 1978; Warren-Rhodes and Koenig, 2001; Huang and Hsu, 2003). Studies of urban metabolism measure inputs, outputs, and material recycling within a city or metropolitan area (Huang and Hsu, 2003). The conversion of diverse physical quantities into units of energy allows for consistent comparisons between cities.

By some accounts, urban metabolism can also be understood more explicitly in terms of sustainability. Mitchell (1998) defines urban metabolism as the 'social as well as biophysical [means]

TABLE 3 Ecological footprint and biocapacity, 2002 data

	Population (million)	Total ecological footprint (global ha/person)	Food, fibre, and timber footprint (global ha/person)	Energy footprint (global ha/person)	Total biocapacity (global ha/person)	Ecological deficit or reserve (global ha/person)
WORLD	6,225.0	2.2	0.9	1.2	1.8	−0.4
High income countries	925.6	6.4	2.1	4.1	3.4	−3.0
Middle income countries	2,989.4	1.9	0.9	0.9	2.1	0.2
Low income countries	2,279.8	0.8	0.5	0.3	0.7	−0.1

Source: European Environment Agency and Global Footprint Network (2005).

by which cities acquire or lose the capacity for sustainability in the face of diverse and competing problems'. By sustainability he means the maintenance of resources and quality of life in the face of hazards and risk. This conception of urban metabolism aligns with the 'ecological footprint' concept pioneered by Mathis Wackernagel and William Rees (Wackernagel and Rees, 1996; Wackernagel et al., 1999). The biologically productive areas that account for an area's footprint are taken to mean the amount of land available to create the low-entropy (highly useful) energy needed to sustain consumption (production plus imports, minus exports) patterns of a given human population, as well as the land capacity needed to assimilate waste products and greenhouse gas emissions (Wackernagel et al., 1999). The ecological footprint offers a common unit for the analysis of consumption patterns, and may thus serve as a complement to energy-based assessments of urban metabolism.

At the scale of a city or region, most of the biologically productive land will be found outside of the system. This realization illuminates the ability of wealthy nations to externalize the effects of higher levels of consumption by both importing resources and exporting wastes, often over tremendous distances. A number of studies have been done to calculate municipal ecological footprints, and the Global Footprint Network produces national ecological footprints, summarized in Table 3. These national studies also calculate 'biocapacity' – the amount of productive land each nation has within its borders – in order to relate consumption to natural resource endowment. On the whole, human society is consuming more materials and energy than are globally available over the long term, shown as an overall global 'ecological deficit'.

Locally, cities are also consuming more than is regionally or globally available over the long term. A study of York, UK, calculated the total ecological footprint of the city to be 1,254,000 ha, yielding an average per capita figure of 6.98 ha (Barrett et al., 2002). This is not only significantly larger than the total land area of York itself, but is higher than the 5.6 ha per capita ecological footprint for the UK and developed nations as a whole, as calculated in 2002 (European Environment Agency and Global Footprint Network, 2005). Just under half of the total amount of materials consumed actually entered the city; the remainder accounted for the production and transportation of goods as well as other hidden energy flows and losses. A second regional study, of the Isle of Wight, found total material consumption to be in excess of 750,000 tonnes (5.8 t per capita) in 1998/1999 (Best Foot Forward, 2000). This consumption resulted in an ecological footprint of 5.15 ha per capita, the majority belonging to the tourist population visiting the region each year.

In general, urbanization increases energy demand as the needs of physical and social infrastructure grows within cities (Huang and Chen, 2005). Much of this increased energy demand has been met with, and indeed facilitated by, the use of fossil fuels (Smil, 1994; Unruh, 2000). The relations between fossil-fuel use and overall urban metabolism is most notable in rapidly developing and urbanizing economies, such as the Democratic Republic of Korea (UNEP, 2003) and India (UNEP, 2001a), where per capita fossil-fuel use across all sectors has increased rapidly over the last decade. A study by Warren-Rhodes and Koenig (2001) of the city of Hong Kong showed significant increases in both consumption and waste outputs between 1970 and 1997. The first urban metabolism study conducted on a North American region was completed in Toronto in 2003, suggesting slow development of the concept (Sahely et al., 2003). This study showed that, in general, inputs (consumption) were increasing more rapidly than outputs (waste). Observed residential solid waste and wastewater outflows decreased in real terms over the study period (1987–1999).

The degree to which an urban area makes responsible use of its regional natural resources – both for the creation of material goods and the assimilation of waste products – has a significant influence on local environmental quality and quality of life. These effects are felt differently within and across countries, as well as across socioeconomic gradients.

3.4. Urban environmental quality

Urbanization means increasing rates of direct and indirect consumption of energy, materials and ecosystem services, as well as significant displacement of natural ecosystems (McGranahan and Marcotullio, 2006). Urban environmental problems, founded upon this appropriation and degradation of natural ecosystem structure and function, as well as stress on social institutions and urban infrastructure, vary regionally and through time as cities develop economically; a number of researchers (e.g. McGranahan et al., 2001) have supplied graphic representations of this phenomenon. As can be seen in Figure 2, local environmental concerns, such as indoor air quality and sanitation, are much more pronounced in rural and low-income urban conditions. These problems are largely driven by development paths characterized by rapid demographic change that do not significantly account for key biological and ecological processes, such as the dynamics of infectious diseases and the provision of ecosystem services. Regional problems, such as declining outdoor air quality, emerge as cities develop and incomes increase. Industrialization and the increased use of private automobiles, characteristic of a development path in larger cities that fails to consider effects on regional ecosystems, are indirect drivers of these problems. More global problems, such as climate change, increase with increasing development and wealth. Excessive material wealth, exaggerated ecological footprints, generation of greenhouse gas emissions and solid waste, and a development path ignorant of (or unconcerned with) the global effects of consumption are driving these changes. The time scale over which these concerns are experienced also changes: with more local concerns posing much more immediate threats to health and well-being; and global problems occurring more slowly, with damage being harder to see, understand and react to. Some of the most serious conditions at present are due to rapid urbanization that is causing more local and immediate environmental health issues (e.g. inadequate sanitation and access to clean drinking water) to be experienced at the same time as more modern, global concerns (e.g. climate change), effectively reducing cities' capacity to respond to all problems.

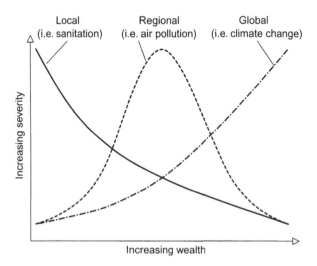

FIGURE 2 Evolution of urban environmental problems (after McGranahan et al., 2001).

4. Understanding the complexity of urban systems

Traditionally, city planning has focused on spatial planning, housing, transport, energy, and water systems to individually and specifically react to, and address the drivers of urban change discussed in Section 3. As the interrelations between individual drivers are becoming increasingly apparent, focus has shifted to the integration of planning and management of land use with physical infrastructure, sociocultural and economic issues, as well as environmental quality. In the process, insights from complexity theory have been proposed as relevant in order to understand and guide the development of cities. Those insights are used in two different, though related, ways.

First, there is the study of cities as complex systems, where the macrobehaviours of cities are modelled and investigated much like the macrobehaviours of chemical or biological systems. The relevant modern conceptualizations of complexity used in this research originate in the work of Ilya Prigogine and co-workers (see, e.g., Prigogine, 1980), who studied open systems – typically physical or chemical systems that were characterized by the exchange of mass and energy across system boundaries. Here, non-equilibrium thermodynamics provided crucial insights into the behaviour of many such systems. As these systems are exposed to changes in energy flows from the outside, structures emerge inside that help dissipate those flows. When stability thresholds are exceeded, the systems may experience a transition to a new structure which, in turn, possesses its own limited development potential (Nicolis and Prigogine, 1977).

The early work on silicones and other materials was soon extended to address the formation of and change in the structure of biological systems, from cells to entire ecosystems (Prigogine et al., 1972). For example, Eric Schneider described

> life itself [a]s a product of the thermodynamic histories of the global ecosystem as it evolved from chemical elements and, through energy flux transformations, developed useful genetic materials that reproduce and metabolize into highly organized systems through stepwise energy transformations (Schneider, 1988, p. 116).

The appeal of complexity theory as a unifying framework to explain system change was further extended, at least by analogy, to shed light on economic growth and development (for a review, see Ruth, 2005). Some have begun to build computer simulation models of social and economic systems which describe them explicitly as non-linear, open, self-organizing systems. Peter Allen (1997), a former student of Prigogine's, has been among the first to do so for urban systems. The urban dynamics simulation models of Jay Forrester (1969), though not explicitly guided by complexity theory, do recognize the importance of system openness, non-linearities and time lags. His models focus on the interplay of physical urban infrastructure, economic development, and pollution in a way that is closely related to the notion of urban metabolism discussed above.

While much of the work on complex systems behaviour has been descriptive or simulation-oriented, lessons from complex systems analysis are slowly beginning to inform policy and investment decision-making. If systems, such as cities, are indeed best described as open, diverse in structure, and varied in interacting components; if, furthermore, many of these interactions are non-linear and time-lagged; and if the components themselves are complex systems nested within other complex systems, then – so the argument goes – a complex systems approach is needed in order to understand and guide their behaviour (Rotmans and van Asselt, 2000; Rotmans, 2006).

Complex systems analysis, thus, has rapidly evolved from a descriptive into a prescriptive endeavour, and in the process has shaped the thinking about, and management of, urban areas. For example, the BEQUEST Project (Bentivegna et al., 2002) has begun to provide insights into the complex social, technical and environmental processes of urban change and offered a framework to structure information on, and intervention into, those processes at levels that span from aggregate regional performance to smaller-scale, subsystem-specific operational issues. Others, such as the CitiesPlus programme launched for Vancouver (CitiesPlus, 2005) have built on the diverse knowledge of stakeholders to develop 100-year urban sustainability plans. The IntelCities programme, supported by the European Union, has expanded the opportunities for information collection and sharing by employing information technology to facilitate the interaction of electronic government, information communication technology (ICT) companies, research groups and citizens across 18 European cities (IntelCities, 2007). In efforts to embrace the complexity of urban change, these and other programmes have frequently encountered the challenges that are inherent when trying to provide 'management advice' on the basis of a world view that emphasizes non-deterministic system behaviour.

As a consequence of complexity, novelty and surprise are unavoidable features of system development (Funtowicz and Ravetz, 1991). One approach to dealing with complexity and uncertainty in a pragmatic fashion is to require that different perspectives on the various system elements and their interactions are provided by different stakeholders from a range of scientific, public, private and non-profit communities (Bond, 1998; Hulme and Taylor, 2000). Several of the integrated urban assessments discussed above have attempted to provide a rich, multidisciplinary perspective, informed – and on occasion guided – by insights from many different stakeholders. Yet, managing the contributions from a large and diverse set of stakeholders has itself become a complex management task. The scarcity of resources for those projects and their inherent short duration of usually only 1–5 years have largely prevented them from becoming institutionalized to a point where they can have any long-reaching policy impact. As a consequence, the extent of stakeholder dialogue and involvement is frequently curtailed to keep projects within resource constraints.

A second means of capturing a wide range of influences on the behaviour of urban systems is to craft scenarios that are consistent both internally and broadly with respect to the contributed viewpoints on the strength and role of outside influences on the system and drivers within the system. Frequently, contrasting scenarios represent the alternative viewpoints of stakeholders. Playing those scenarios out – often with the help of computer models – and interpreting their consequences across sectors and across time can provide a valuable input for institutional learning. Furthermore, to the extent that the primary elements of an urban system are formally modelled, the quantitative (and qualitative) outputs from simulation exercises can be used to inform feedbacks between system response and intervention through investment and policy choice, as indicated in Figure 2.

Computer models of complex urban dynamics can improve, iteratively, the knowledge of stakeholders, and with that knowledge perhaps improve decision-makers' ability to influence those dynamics. It is in this sense that adaptive management (Holling, 1978; Gunderson et al., 1995) can be a key element in problem-solving. However, an added challenge in urban planning and management that is not present in many of the other areas to which adaptive management has been applied, lies in the lumpiness and irreversibility of infrastructure investments. Long lead times and lifetimes of projects in many ways prevent adaptation – once an urban highway system is put in place or an underground sewer network has been laid, changes are virtually impossible. Here it becomes even more important to explore, in structured and quantifiable ways, the potential future implications of current investment and policy choices. Implementing more anticipatory management (Ruth, 2006b) is proving to be even more of a challenge than establishing adaptive management as a guiding principle for investment and policy-making.

5. Summary and conclusions

In this article we reflected on the drivers of urban change, and various approaches to understanding and managing that change. While the research areas in urban theory and analysis are broad, we have deliberately focused on recent developments that were spawned by, or are otherwise closely related to, insights from complexity theory, and that are part of the ongoing discussion about the impacts of global (environmental) change on quality of life in cities. We argued that continued urbanization, more extensive globalization, and increasing impacts of global environmental change pose complex challenges to urban planners and managers and require that the scientific community develops and uses concepts and methods that advance the understanding of that complexity. This is particularly important if the science is used to inform policy and investment decision-making.

Yet, as urban analysis begins to integrate insights about the complex behaviour of urban systems and uses frameworks for analysis, either explicitly or implicitly, that are informed by complexity theory, several challenges emerge. First, there is the problem of mismatched world views: decision-makers are asking for projections on which to base their decisions; integrated assessments provide diverse scenarios of potential future system trajectories. Rather than basing decisions on projections, the challenge will be to identify strategies that are robust for a wide range of possible scenarios. Second, and closely related to the first of these challenges: for one group, models and reports are an end product that (linearly) enters into a decision-making process; for the other, integrated assessment is part of an iterative process of adaptive and anticipatory management. Given limited budgets and planning horizons, adaptive and anticipatory management are difficult to implement in many institutional settings.

Efforts to address these challenges are themselves rife with problems. Embracing broad stakeholder communities in the scientific process can bias the science through the undue influence of special interests. It can also reduce the value that science adds to the decision-making process if it must meet some lower common denominator during the consensus-building process, for example if only a narrow set of scenarios are presented to scope investment and policy choices, or if the creation of scenarios itself is strongly biased towards pre-existing notions of what the future *will* look like. Current environmental research points as much to the complexity of the decision-making process itself, as it contributes to the understanding of complex relationships among urban infrastructure, population and institutions. The biggest challenge may well lie in the innovation of institutions that plan for, and manage, urban dynamics.

However, as the number, breadth and depth of case studies of urban change increase, and as the climate change community turns its attention – and with it some of its intellectual and financial resources – to cities, theoretical and practical experience will, no doubt, accumulate to help overcome many of these challenges. The next major frontier may be integration simultaneously along three dimensions – first, an integration of theoretical, empirical and simulation-based assessments; second, the integration of research and stakeholder knowledge for the application to location-specific issues; and third, the integration of knowledge generated from those applications into a new theory of, and management approach to, complex urban change.

References

Allen, P.M., 1997, *Cities and Regions as Self-organizing Systems: Models of Complexity*, Gordon and Breach Science Publishers, Amsterdam.

Arthur, W.B., 1989, 'Competing technologies, increasing returns, and lock-in by historical events', *Economic Journal* 99(394), 116–131.

ASCE, 2005, *Report Card for America's Infrastructure*, American Society of Civil Engineers [available at www.asce.org/reportcard/2005/index.cfm].

Barrett, J., Vallack, H., Jones, A., Haq, G., 2002, *A Material Flow Analysis and Ecological Footprint of York*, Stockholm Environment Institute, Stockholm.

Batty, M., 2005, *Cities and Complexity: Understanding Cities with Cellular Automata, Agent-based Models, and Fractals*, MIT Press, Cambridge, MA.

Bentivegna, V., Curwell, S., Deakin, M., Lombardi, P., Mitchell, G., Nijkamp, P., 2002, A vision and methodology for integrated sustainable urban development, *Building Research and Information* 30(2), 83–94.

Best Foot Forward, 2000, *Island State: An Ecological Footprint Analysis of the Isle of Wight* [available at www.bestfootforward.com/reports.html].

Black, D., Henderson, V., 1999, 'The theory of urban growth', *Journal of Political Economy* 107(2), 252–284.

Bloomfield, J., Smith, M., Thompson, N., 1999, *Hot Nights in the City: Global Warming, Sea-Level Rise and the New York Metropolitan Region*, Environmental Defense Fund, Washington, DC.

Bond, R., 1998, *Lessons for the Large-scale Application of Process Approaches from Sri Lanka*, Gate Keeper Series 75, International Institute for Environment and Development (IIED), London.

Brenner, N., 2000, 'The urban question: reflections on Henri Lefebvre, urban theory and the politics of scale', *International Journal of Urban and Regional Research* 24(2), 361.

Camagni, R., Capello, R., Nijkamp, P., 1998, 'Towards sustainable city policy: an economy: environment technology nexus', *Ecological Economics* 24(1), 103–118.

CitiesPlus, 2005, *CitiesPlus* [available at www.citiesplus.ca/].

Cohen, B., 2004, 'Urban growth in developing countries: a review of current trends and a caution regarding existing forecasts', *World Development* 32(1), 23–51.

Curwell, S.R., Deakin, M., 2002, Sustainable urban development and BEQUEST, *Building Research and Information* 30(2), 79-82.

Davison, R., Vogel, D., Harris, R., Jones, N., 2000, 'Technology leapfrogging in developing countries: an inevitable luxury?', *Electronic Journal on Information Systems in Developing Countries* 1(5), 1–10.

Dear, M.J., Dishman, J.D., 2002, *From Chicago to L.A.: Making Sense of Urban Theory*, Sage Publications, Thousand Oaks, CA.

EAI, 2005, *SimCity Societies*, Electronic Arts Inc. [available at http://simcity.ea.com/].

European Commission, 2006, *Energy, Environment and Sustainable Development: The City of Tomorrow and Cultural Heritage*, The European Commission [available at http://ec.europa.eu/research/eesd/leaflets/en/keyact04.html].

European Environment Agency, 1998, *Europe's Environment: The Second Assessment*, State of the Environment Report No 2, European Environment Agency, Copenhagen [available at http://reports.eea.europa.eu/92-828-3351-8/en].

European Environment Agency and Global Footprint Network, 2005, *National Ecological Footprint and Biocapacity Accounts*, 2005 Edition [available at www.footprintnetwork.org].

Forrester, J.W., 1969, *Urban Dynamics*, Productivity Press, Portland, OR.

Fujita, M., Krugman, P., Venables, A.J., 1999, *The Spatial Economy: Cities, Regions, and International Trade*, MIT Press, Cambridge, MA.

Funtowicz, S.O., Ravetz, J.R., 1991, 'A new scientific methodology for global environmental issues', in: R. Costanza (ed.), *Ecological Economics: The Science and Management of Sustainability*, Columbia University Press, New York.

Golob, T.F., Regan, A.C., 2001, 'Impacts of information technology on personal travel and commercial vehicle operations: research challenges and opportunities', *Transportation Research, Part C – Emerging Technologies* 9, 87–121.

Graham, S., Marvin, S., 1996, *Telecommunications and the City*, Routledge, New York.

Gunderson, L., Holling, C.S., Light, S. (eds), 1995, *Barriers and Bridges to the Renewal of Ecosystems and Institutions*, Columbia University Press, New York.

Guy, S., 1996, 'Managing water stress: the logic of demand side infrastructure planning', *Journal of Environmental Planning and Management* 39(1), 123–130.

Healey, P., 2007, *Urban Complexity and Spatial Strategies: Towards a Relational Planning for Our Times*, Routledge, London.

Holling, C.S. (ed.), 1978, *Adaptive Environmental Assessment and Management*, Wiley, Chichester, UK.

Holman, I.P., Rounsevell, M.D.A., Shackley, S., Harrison, P.A., Nicholls, R.J., Berry, P.M., Audsley, E., 2005a, 'A regional, multi-sectoral and integrated assessment of the impacts of climate and socio-economic change in the UK. Part I. Methodology', *Climatic Change* 71, 9–41.

Holman, I.P., Nicholls, R.J., Berry, P.M., Harrison, P.A., Audsley, E., Shackley, S., Rounsevell, M.D.A., 2005b, 'A regional, multi-sectoral and integrated assessment of the impacts of climate and socio-economic change in the UK. Part II. Results', *Climatic Change* 71, 43–73.

Hoo, W., Sumitani, M., 2005, *Climate Change Will Impact the Seattle Department of Transportation*, Office of the City Auditor, August 2005, Seattle, WA.

Huang, S.-L., Chen, C.-W., 2005, 'Theory of urban energetics and mechanisms of urban development', *Ecological Modelling* 189, 49–71.

Huang, S.-L., Hsu, W.-L., 2003, 'Materials flow analysis and emergy evaluation of Taipei's urban construction', *Landscape and Urban Planning* 63, 61–74.

Hulme, D., Taylor, R., 2000, 'Integrating environmental, economic and social appraisal in the real world: from impact assessment to adaptive management', in: N. Lee, C. Kirkpatrick (eds), *Integrated Appraisal and Sustainable Development in a Developing World*, Edward Elgar, Cheltenham, UK.

IHDP, 2001, *Industrial Transformation*, International Human Dimensions Programme [available at http://130.37.129.100/ivm/research/ihdp-it/it_publications/IHDP-IT_project_sept2001.pdf].

IntelCities, 2007, *About the IntelCities Project* [available at www.iti.gr/intelcities].

Jollands, N., Ruth, M., Bernier, C., Golubiewski, N., Andrew, R., Forgie, V., 2005, *Climate's Long-term Impacts on New Zealand Infrastructure*, Phase I Report, Hamilton City Case Study, New Zealand Centre for Ecological Economics, Massey University, Palmerston North, New Zealand, and School of Public Policy, University of Maryland, College Park, MD.

Jollands, N, Andrew, R., Ruth, M., Ahmad, S., London, M., Lennox, J., Bartleet, M., 2006, *Climate's Long-term Impacts on New Zealand Infrastructure*, Phase II Report, Wellington City Case Study, New Zealand Centre for Ecological Economics, Massey University, Palmerston North, New Zealand, and Center for Integrative Environmental Research, University of Maryland, College Park, MD.

Kirshen, P.H., Ruth, M., Anderson, W., Lakshmanan, T.R., Chapra, S., Chudyk, W., Edgers, L., Gute, D., Sanayei, M., Vogel, R., 2004, *Climate's Long-term Impacts on Metro Boston*, Final Report to the US Environmental Protection Agency, Office of Research and Development, Washington, DC.

Koteen, L., Bloomfield, J., Eichler, T., Tonne, C., Young, R., Poulshock, H., Sosler, A., 2001, *Hot Prospects: The Potential Impacts of Global Warming on Los Angeles and the Southland*, Environmental Defense Fund, Washington, DC.

Lange, H., Garrelts, H., 2006, *Integrated Flood Risk Management in an Individualised Society (INNIG) Within the Scope of the BMBF Programme on "Risk Management of Extreme Flood Occasions"*, University of Bremen Research Center for Sustainability Studies (ARTEC) [available at www.artec.uni-bremen.de/eng/projects/showProject.php?id=17].

McGranahan, G., Marcotullio, P., 2006, 'Urban systems', in: R. Hassan, R. Scholes, N. Ash (eds), *Ecosystems and Human Well-being: Current State and Trends, Volume 1*, Millennium Ecosystem Assessment, United Nations Environment Program, Island Press, Washington, DC.

McGranahan, G., Jacobi, P., Songsore, J., Surjadi, C., Kjellén,M., 2001, *The Citizens at Risk: From Urban Sanitation to Sustainable Cities*, Earthscan, London.

Mitchell, J.K., 1998, 'Urban metabolism and disaster vulnerability in an era', in: H.-J. Schellnhuber, V. Wenzel (eds), *Earth System Analysis: Integrating Science for Sustainability*, Springer, Berlin, 359–377.

Newcombe, K., Kalma, J., Aston, A., 1978, 'The metabolism of a city: the case of Hong Kong', *Ambio* 7, 3–15.

Newton, P., 2001, *Australia State of the Environment 2001*, CSIRO Publishing, Collingwood, Australia.

Nicolis, G., Prigogine, I., 1977, *Self-Organization in Non-Equilibrium Systems*, John Wiley and Sons, New York.

Nijkamp, P., Reggiani, A. (eds), 1992, *Interaction, Evolution, and Chaos in Space*, Springer, Berlin.

NSF, 1997, *Understanding Urban Interactions: Summary of a Research Workshop*, US National Science Foundation, Arlington, VA.

NSF, 2000, *Towards a Comprehensive Geographical Perspective on Urban Sustainability*, Final Report of the 1998 National Science Foundation Workshop on Urban Sustainability [available at http://citeseer.ist.psu.edu/hanson00towards.html].

OECD, 1993, *Core Set of Indicators for Environmental Performance Review*, Environmental Monograph No. 83, Organization for Economic Cooperation and Development, Paris.

Prigogine, I., 1980, *From Being to Becoming: Time and Complexity in the Physical Sciences*, W.H. Freeman and Company, New York.

Prigogine, I., Nicolis, G., Babloyantz, A., 1972, 'A thermodynamics of evolution', *Physics Today* 23, 23–28.

Robson, B.T., 1969, *Urban Analysis: A Study of City Structure*, Cambridge University Press, Cambridge, UK.

Rosenzweig, C., Solecki, W., Paine, C., Gornitz, V., Hartig, E., Jacob, K., Major, D., Kinney, P., Hill, D., Zimmerman, R., 2000, *Climate Change and a Global City: An Assessment of the Metropolitan East Coast Region*, US Global Change Research Program [available at http://metroeast_climate.ciesin.columbia.edu].

Rotmans, J., 1994, *Global Change and Sustainable Development: A Modelling Perspective for the Next Decade*, National Institute of Public Health and Environmental Protection, Bilthoven, The Netherlands.

Rotmans, J., 2006, 'A complex systems approach for sustainable cities', in: M. Ruth (ed.), *Smart Growth and Climate Change: Regional Development, Infrastructure and Adaptation*, Edward Elgar, Cheltenham, UK, 155–180.

Rotmans, J., van Asselt, M.B.A., 2000, 'Towards an integrated approach for sustainable city planning', *Journal on Multi-Criteria Decision Analysis* 9, 110–124.

Ruth, M., 2005, 'Insights from thermodynamics for the analysis of economic processes', in: A. Kleidon, R.D. Lorenz (eds), *Non-Equilibrium Thermodynamics and the Production of Entropy*, Springer, Heidelberg, Germany, 243–254.

Ruth, M. (ed.), 2006a, *Smart Growth and Climate Change*, Edward Elgar, Cheltenham, UK.

Ruth, M., 2006b, 'The economics of sustainability and the sustainability of economics', *Ecological Economics* 56(3), 332–342.

Sahely, H.R., Dudding, S., Kennedy, C.A., 2003, 'Estimating the urban metabolism of Canadian Cities: Greater Toronto Area case study', *Canadian Journal of Civil Engineering* 30, 468–483.

Schneider, E.D., 1988, 'Thermodynamics, ecological succession, and natural selection: a common thread', in: B.H. Weber, D.J. Depew, J.D. Smith (eds), *Entropy, Information, and Evolution*, MIT Press, Cambridge, MA, 107–138.

Smil, V., 1994, *Energy in World History*, Westview Press, Boulder, CO.

UNDP, 2003, *Human Development Indicators 2003*, United Nations Development Program, Washington, DC [available at http://hdr.undp.org/reports/global/2003/indicator/indic_38_1_2.html].

UNEP, 2001a, *The State of the Environment – India: 2001*, United Nations Environment Program, Washington, DC [available at http://envfor.nic.in/soer/2001/soer.html].

UNEP, 2001b, *State of Environment Lao PDR 2001*, United Nations Environment Program, Washington, DC [available at http://ekh.unep.org/?q=node/287].

UNEP, 2001c, *State of Environment, Sri Lanka 2001*, United Nations Environment Program, Washington, DC [available at www.rrcap.unep.org/reports/soe/srilankasoe.cfm].

UNEP, 2003, *State of the Environment DPR Korea 2003*, United Nations Environment Program, Washington, DC [available at www.unep.org/PDF/DPRK_SOE_Report.pdf].

Unruh, G., 2000, 'Understanding carbon lock-in', *Energy Policy* 28, 817–830.

Unruh, G., 2002, 'Escaping carbon lock-in', *Energy Policy* 30(4), 317–325.

Urri, J., 2000, *Sociology Beyond Societies: Mobilities for the Twenty-first Century*, Routledge, London.

Wackernagel, M., Rees, W., 1996, *Our Ecological Footprint: Reducing Human Impact on the Earth*, New Society Publishers, Gabriola Island, BC, Canada.

Wackernagel, M., Onisto, L., Bello, P., Callejas Linares, A., López Falfán, I., Méndez García, J., Suárez Guerrero, A., Suárez Guerrero, G., 1999, 'National capital accounting with the ecological footprint concept', *Ecological Economics* 29, 375–390.

Warren-Rhodes, K., Koenig, A., 2001, 'Escalating trends in the urban metabolism of Hong Kong: 1971–1997', *Ambio* 30(7), 429–438.

World Bank, 2006, *World Development Report: Equity and Development*, The World Bank and Oxford University Press, Washington, DC.

■ synthesis article

Vulnerability, poverty and the need for sustainable adaptation measures

SIRI H. ERIKSEN*, KAREN O'BRIEN

Department of Sociology and Human Geography, University of Oslo, PO Box 1096 Blindern, 0317 Oslo, Norway

The need to address both poverty *and* vulnerability to climate change can be considered two of the major challenges facing human society in the 21st century. While the two concepts are closely interconnected, they are nonetheless distinct. A conceptual understanding of the relationship between vulnerability and poverty is presented, and the types of responses that can address both of these challenges are identified. An empirical example from Kenya is used to show how climate change adaptation can potentially reconcile the objectives of both poverty reduction and vulnerability reduction. Significantly, each and every poverty reduction measure does not reduce vulnerability to climate change, just as each and every adaptation measure does not automatically contribute to poverty reduction. It is argued that adaptation measures need to specifically target vulnerability–poverty linkages. Although most adaptation efforts have been focused on reducing risk, there is a need to address local capacity to adapt, as well as the societal processes generating vulnerability. An implication is that the mode of implementing adaptation measures must capture the specificity of both the vulnerability and poverty context. Furthermore, adaptation is not simply a local activity, since targeting the processes generating vulnerability and poverty often entails addressing political and economic structures.

Keywords: adaptation; capacity building; climate change; developing countries; governance; Kenya; poverty; risk reduction; sustainable development; vulnerability

La pauvreté, aussi bien que la vulnérabilité au changement climatique, représentent deux des plus gros défis pour la société humaine du 21ème siècle. Bien que les deux concepts soient intimement liés, ils sont toutefois distincts. Une compréhension d'ordre conceptuelle de la relation entre vulnérabilité et pauvreté est présentée, et les catégories d'actions pouvant aborder les deux problèmes ensemble sont identifiées. Un exemple empirique au Kenya est employé pour illustrer comment l'adaptation aux changements climatiques pourrait concilier les objectifs de réduction de la pauvreté et de la vulnérabilité. Notoirement, toute mesure de lutte contre la pauvreté n'agit pas nécessairement sur la vulnérabilité au changement climatique, tout comme toute mesure d'adaptation n'aide pas forcément à lutter contre la pauvreté. Nous postulons que les mesures d'adaptation doivent spécifiquement viser les liens entre la pauvreté et la vulnérabilité. Bien que la majeure partie des mesures d'adaptation aient été axée sur la réduction des risques, il faut prendre en compte les capacités locales d'adaptation, ainsi que les procédés sociaux à l'origine de la vulnérabilité. Une des conséquences est que le mode d'application des mesures d'adaptation doit intégrer les spécificités du contexte de pauvreté et de vulnérabilité. De plus, l'adaptation n'est pas qu'une activité locale, étant donné le besoin d'incorporer les structure politiques et économiques dans la prise en compte des processus a l'origine de la vulnérabilité et de la pauvreté.

Mots clés: adaptation; changement climatique; développement durable; gouvernance; Kenya; pauvreté; pays en développement; réduction des risques; renforcement des capacitives; vulnérabilité

■ *Corresponding author. E-mail*: siri.eriksen@sgeo.uio.no

CLIMATE POLICY **7 (2007) 337–352**

1. Introduction

It is widely recognized that a reduction in both poverty and inequality is necessary for sustainable development to be achieved (Christoff, 1996; Watson, 2002; Costanza, 2003). At the same time, there is now little doubt that climate change will influence livelihoods and development trajectories over the coming decades. Like poverty reduction, reducing vulnerability to climate change through adaptation measures is increasingly seen as a prerequisite for sustainable development (Cohen et al., 1998; Christie and Hanlon, 2001; Markandya and Halsnæs, 2002; Swart et al., 2003; Agrawala, 2004; Klein et al., 2007; Yohe et al., 2007). Addressing both poverty *and* vulnerability to climate change are two of the major challenges to sustainable development in the 21st century.

Poverty and vulnerability to climate change are, however, not identical problems that are automatically addressed together. Poverty contributes to vulnerability, and vulnerability to climate change often leads to outcomes that perpetuate poverty. Assuming that responses that reduce poverty will similarly reduce vulnerability to climate change may lead to policies and programs that create contradictory outcomes: poverty reduction as pursued by efforts to meet the Millennium Development Goals (MDGs) may in some cases increase vulnerability to climate change, which in turn may perpetuate or increase poverty. As one example, the promotion of economic development through shrimp farming may enhance incomes, but it may also contribute to the loss of wetlands and mangroves and increase vulnerability to cyclones, which can have disastrous effects on livelihoods and hence exacerbate poverty (Adger et al., 2005).

In this article, we present a conceptual understanding of the relationship between poverty and vulnerability, and identify the types of responses that can address both of these challenges. The discussion focuses on developing countries, where the overlaps between poverty and vulnerability to climate change are arguably the most pronounced. We then draw upon an empirical example from Kenya to show how the objectives of both poverty reduction and vulnerability reduction can potentially be reconciled through sustainable adaptation measures. A key message is that although the high vulnerability of poor people to climate change provides a justification for interventions, not any and every adaptation measure automatically reduces vulnerability of the poor, or contributes to poverty reduction in the face of climate change. Likewise, not all poverty reduction measures reduce vulnerability to climate change; in some cases they may increase vulnerability and pose new threats to well-being. Unless policies and interventions are specifically targeted at (1) reducing the risks posed by climate change to the way that people secure their own well-being; (2) enhancing the adaptive capacity of the poor; and (3) confronting the processes that generate vulnerability, they may undermine sustainable development. Policies and interventions should focus on the areas of overlap between poverty and vulnerability, i.e. on adaptation measures that reduce *both* poverty and vulnerability to climate change. This interface between vulnerability reduction and poverty reduction measures can be considered to be 'sustainable adaptation'.

2. Conceptual framework: vulnerability–poverty linkages

Vulnerability is a concept that is widely used in the natural hazards, food security and climate change communities, yet there are diverse definitions and interpretations (Chambers, 1989; Wisner et al., 2004; Füssel and Klein, 2006; O'Brien et al., 2007). In general, it refers to the likelihood of injury, death, loss, disruption of livelihoods or other harm as the result of environmental shocks, such as floods, earthquakes or other hazards, or harm resulting from social changes such as conflict or economic restructuring. Vulnerability to climate variability and change is closely related to the dynamic social, economic, political, institutional, technological and environmental conditions that characterize a particular context and contribute to negative outcomes (Kelly and Adger, 2000; O'Brien et al., 2007). Climate change poses risks to life, livelihoods and well-being for some individuals and groups. One important dimension of vulnerability is the physical risks that result from climate stresses. These stresses include increased surface temperatures, sea-level rise, decreased or increased precipitation, soil erosion, fluctuating and changing courses of rivers, changes in frequency and intensity of storms, changing weather patterns, including drought and flood patterns, and glacier lake outbursts from increased melting of ice-capped mountains (Parry et al., 2007). They represent risks to poor people that are much broader than simply a threat to lives; they can contribute to a failure to secure well-being.

A second dimension of vulnerability is the capacity of people exposed to climate change to cope with and adapt to these risks. Adaptation has been defined as the 'adjustment in ecological, social, or economic systems in response to actual or expected climatic stimuli and their effects or impacts' (Smit and Pilifosova, 2001, p. 881). The entitlement and livelihoods literatures have focused on people's ability to cope with climatic variability in the short term, which can lead to adjustments in the long term (Sen, 1981; Davies, 1993; Glantz, 1994; Scoones et al., 1996; Eakin, 2006). In practice, responses to present-day climate variability present a useful starting point for adapting to future climate change (Burton et al., 2002). For the purpose of this discussion, we consider the ability to cope with climate variability and extreme events as an important facet of adaptive capacity.

A third dimension of vulnerability is the social and environmental processes that exacerbate risks and limit adaptive capacity. Vulnerability is generated by multiple processes, such as social relations of resource access, political and economic marginalization, loss of employment opportunities, and weakening social networks (Adams et al., 1998; Adger and Kelly, 1999).

Since these elements are context-specific, vulnerability varies between individuals and social groups, as well as over time. Vulnerability is thus a dynamic concept; it is in a continuous state of flux as the biophysical and social processes that shape local conditions and ability to cope also change (Handmer et al., 1999; Leichenko and O'Brien, 2002; Eriksen et al., 2005; Thomas and Twyman, 2005).

Many of the processes that generate vulnerability to climate change are closely associated with poverty (Burton et al., 2002; AfDB et al., 2003). Poverty has been described as an extreme deprivation of basic capabilities and well-being (Sen, 1999; UNEP/IISD, 2004). Poverty has also been characterized as a lack of sense of community and/or solidarity, the sense of lacking freedom and rights, feelings of insecurity in the face of natural disasters, violence or economic upheavals, and an inability to influence one's own situation. In this article, we focus on the OECD/DAC definition, which characterizes poverty as the lack of opportunities for people to meet economic, social and other standards of well-being (OECD, 2001). This lack of opportunities can be broken down into four basic categories relating to economic, political, human and social capabilities. These include the capacity to (1) earn an income and meet material needs; (2) speak up for oneself and have rights; (3) maintain health and a basic education; and (4) maintain a sense of social and cultural affiliation. Here, these four categories constitute the ability to secure an individual or group's well-being. This definition of poverty is much broader than an income-based interpretation, which is often simplistically captured by consumption indicators such as the US$1 per day poverty line (OECD, 2001). The discussion focuses mainly on those who are extremely deprived in terms of these four categories (for example, many rural smallholders in sub-Saharan Africa), although we recognize that others may be considered relatively deprived within their local context.

Poverty can be closely linked to all the three dimensions of vulnerability to climate change, i.e. risks to human life and activities, adaptive capacity and the processes generating vulnerability. Yet there is no one-to-one mapping between poverty and climate change vulnerability. One may be wealthy and vulnerable to climate change (e.g. living in high-risk, uninsured areas), or one may be poor and not vulnerable to climate change (e.g. able to use traditional knowledge to adapt to changing conditions) (Tol et al., 2004; Lind and Eriksen, 2006; Schipper and Pelling, 2006). It has been observed both in South Africa and Mexico, for example, that some relatively higher-income farmers practising irrigated agriculture are vulnerable to climate and market risks because they are constrained from diversifying their livelihoods (Eakin, 2006; Ziervogel et al., 2006). Furthermore, not all poor people are vulnerable in the same ways. Poor people differ in their livelihood strategies, social and political relations, and the types of stressors to which they are exposed. As explained by Coetzee:

> ...[P]overty and vulnerability do not coincide in the same way in all cases. People experiencing vulnerability are not necessarily poor; and amongst the poor, there may be varying levels and patterns of vulnerability – depending on the multitude of dynamic processes through which individuals and households respond to changes in the environment, adopt and adjust strategies, and reconfigure their relative well-being (2002, p. 5).

A distinction between poverty and vulnerability implies that there is no 'one-size-fits-all' response to poverty and climate change. For any particular case, the conditions and processes that create poverty may not be the same as those that create vulnerability. However, this is not to say that there are no areas of overlap between poverty and vulnerability. In some cases, poverty and vulnerability to climate change are closely related. Poor people are often the ones to suffer injury, loss, death, or harm from climatic events, and they have less capacity to recover (Kahn, 2005).

Figure 1 represents the relationship between poverty and vulnerability. Processes contributing to the four categories of poverty (described above) are represented by the top left circle. The social and environmental context that contributes to climate change vulnerability is represented by the top right circle. The links between poverty and vulnerability can be found where the two top circles overlap, represented by the shaded area. The size of the overlap will vary, depending on the particular context. For some individuals, groups, regions or countries, there may be a larger area of overlap between poverty and vulnerability than for others. The overlap is identified conceptually by the linkages between the definitions of vulnerability and poverty. That is, the overlap is defined by the factors that lead to failure to secure well-being in the context of climate-related stresses. Based on the three dimensions of vulnerability discussed above, three types of linkages can be identified:

1. *Risk* – Any added risk to current ways of securing well-being resulting from climate change.
2. *Adaptive capacity* – The particular strategies of poor people for coping or adapting in the face of climate stresses.
3. *Processes* – The causes of vulnerability, or specific factors and conditions that make poor people vulnerable to climate stress, or which can push people into destitution.

There are currently numerous international initiatives aimed at reducing poverty and vulnerability to climate change. Poverty reduction measures (bottom left circle) involve responses that range from promoting economic growth to increasing institutional capacity, securing livelihoods, empowering the poor, and increasing freedoms (Sen, 1999; CPRC, 2004; Øyen, 2005; Sachs, 2005).

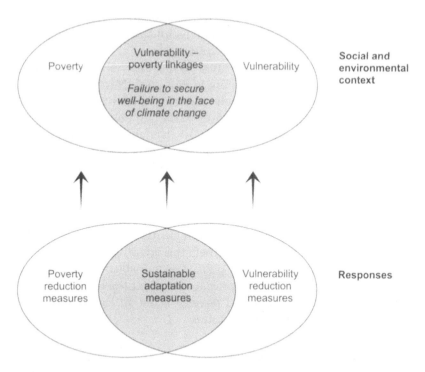

FIGURE 1 Conceptual overview of vulnerability–poverty linkages and sustainable adaptation measures.

Although economic growth is considered by many to be an essential tool for poverty reduction (Dollar and Kraay, 2004; Sachs, 2005), this strategy has been increasingly criticized because it tends to ignore non-material or non-income aspects of poverty, and the processes of exclusion and marginalization that generate poverty. The transition from poverty into a more secure, sustained, non-vulnerable state of well-being often fails when the social, economic and political conditions that create uncertainty and insecurity are not removed (Wood, 2003; Adato et al., 2006). Existing efforts aimed at poverty reduction include the World Bank-driven poverty reduction strategy papers to be implemented at a national level, as well as the UN Millennium Development Goals, which seek greater international commitment to reduce poverty through an increase in aid from developed countries (Sachs, 2005).

Vulnerability reduction measures (bottom right circle) may include responses that reduce biophysical risks as well as addressing the social and environmental factors that influence well-being and people's active strategies to secure this in the face of climate change. International initiatives such as the national adaptation programmes of action (NAPAs) of the UN Framework Convention on Climate Change (UNFCCC) aim to reduce climate change vulnerability in the least developed countries (LDCs). There is also growing interest in identifying ways to mainstream climate change adaptation into development action; that is, to integrate climate change into existing and future development policies and plans (AfDB et al., 2003; Klein et al., 2007) and to use disaster risk reduction to adapt to climate change (O'Brien et al., 2006; Schipper and Pelling, 2006; Thomalla et al., 2006). However, institutional responses seldom draw attention to the role of livelihoods, entitlements and political economy in explaining why the outcomes of climate variability and change are worse or better for some people than for others. There remains a contrast between strategies by individuals and households to cope and adapt, often relying on multiple sources of security, and the more sectoral and technical interventions promoted by national and international institutions (Thomalla et al., 2006; Klein et al., 2007).

Responses aimed at vulnerability reduction often have similar objectives as responses aimed at poverty reduction, i.e. to improve the well-being of the poor. Nevertheless, they each approach the problem from different angles and through different institutional mechanisms. In order to simultaneously address both vulnerability and poverty through policy responses and interventions, it is necessary to identify those measures that target the overlap between vulnerability and poverty (shaded area, top circles). The overlapping responses (shaded area, bottom circles) can be described as 'sustainable adaptation measures' because they secure well-being in the face of climate change. Such responses recognize that reducing vulnerability, poverty and inequality are all important components of sustainable pathways of development (Cohen et al., 1998; Schipper and Pelling, 2006). In line with the three specific linkages between vulnerability and poverty identified above, policy responses should target the shaded area by focusing on measures to (1) reduce risks to current ways of securing well-being; (2) strengthen the adaptive capacity of the poor; and (3) address the causes of vulnerability among the poor. A sustainable adaptation measure may focus on one of these linkages, as long as it does not negatively affect the other two. Below, we elaborate on the relationship between vulnerability and poverty using an example from Kenya, and then discuss examples of sustainable adaptation measures.

3. Identifying vulnerability–poverty linkages

In this section, we present an empirical case that focuses on household responses to drought in a dryland area of Kitui in eastern Kenya, in order to illustrate practical linkages between vulnerability and poverty. We take the ways that poor people secure well-being as a starting point for examining how climate risk, adaptive capacity and societal processes generating vulnerability are linked to both vulnerability and poverty. The discussion is based on a decade of research by one of the authors on household strategies in response to drought (Eriksen et al. 2005, 2006a, 2006b, 2006c; Owuor et al., 2005; Lind and Eriksen 2006). Households in this area consist mainly of small-scale agro-pastoralists who cultivate maize and a mixture of other crops, as well as rearing livestock and engaging in a number of non-agricultural livelihood activities. One also finds nomadic pastoralists in the eastern and southern parts of this district. Droughts are relatively frequent, but floods also represent a climate risk. For example, the 2004–2006 drought was followed by torrential rains and floods in late 2006. The case of Kitui illustrates that in a local vulnerability context, the three poverty–vulnerability linkages of risk, adaptive capacity and causes of vulnerability interact closely with each other.

Household strategies to maintain good health and achieve education for the children form important elements of securing well-being. Access to social infrastructure such as health clinics and schools is, however, difficult in this area. There are few facilities, especially in the drier pastoralist parts of the district. In addition, the cost of school fees, uniforms and necessary school equipment is high relative to incomes. Many poorer households rely mainly on household members securing casual employment on local farms to cover primary school expenses. Casual employment, however, is far from sufficient to pay for secondary schooling, which often involves boarding and travel, and bursaries are few and extremely difficult to get even for the brightest students. Similarly, accessing health clinics involves long travel for many, and upon arrival there are long queues and few qualified staff. Medical bills are often a huge burden on households, necessitating the sale of food stocks, poultry or livestock, or the pursuit of casual employment instead of attending to their own farms. As is common elsewhere in Africa, people use local medicinal plants and seek advice from herbalists in order to treat many illnesses, because these are trusted and may be available closer to home (Bowen et al., 2003; Eriksen et al., 2006a).

Droughts and floods aggravate the difficulties people experience in securing health and education needs. Floods destroy schools and other infrastructure, cut off roads, and make facilities even more difficult to access. During the seasonal rains, Kitui hospital cannot be reached by road from many parts of the district. During the severe floods in late 2006, many villages were isolated by overflowing rivers that could not be crossed on foot, let alone by public or motorized transport. Droughts provide a different set of challenges. Payment of school fees also often coincides with the dry season and low food stocks, when money is short. Children, especially those in poorer households, often drop out of school during droughts because they are too hungry or because they are needed to assist their parents in alternative livelihood options, either by searching for wild foods in the forest, or by engaging in casual employment and petty trade. Poor water supply during droughts has in several instances led to unsanitary conditions and the spread of disease (Eriksen et al., 2005).

Climate stress hence represents a risk to people's strategies to secure their well-being, and it represents a risk to the infrastructure and resources that are important for the success of such strategies. However, it could be argued that it is the poor coverage and state of the infrastructure in the first place, rather than the drought or flood in itself, that is the underlying cause of vulnerability and a failure to secure well-being in the face of climate stress. Socio-economic marginalization and powerlessness (including difficulties in organizing and bargaining, lack of influence and lack of independence) represent important aspects of poverty and are also processes that generate vulnerability among the poor in Kitui. In addition to a lack of influence over development decisions, or inability to lodge complaints regarding lack of government services such as water provision, a lack of rights in the area has been manifested in exclusion from decision-making regarding government gazettement for conservation of a forest, which denies the local population access to resources (such as water, livestock grazing lands and forest products) that are crucial for securing livelihoods during droughts (Owuor et al., 2005). Droughts have sometimes been used politically to buy loyalties. People who are poor and dependent on aid during droughts (and who are threatened with withdrawal of aid if they do not vote for the government) may therefore, in practice, lose important democratic rights. Economic marginalization of dryland farmers in Kenya is manifested in, for example, the vague legal status of important income sources during droughts. In the case of charcoal production, many of the proceeds are captured by traders and police checkpoints, pushing down producer prices and investment to a minimum (Bailis et al., 2006).

Existing power relations at the village level also pervade socially differentiated drought outcomes. Households that are members of clans with powerful political positions, relative wealth and highly skilled jobs can more effectively be assisted (with food, money or employment) by other clan members when a drought wipes out their crop than a household belonging to a weak clan, for example. Within clans, too, outcomes may be differentiated during drought, since a woman who is married into a clan sometimes assumes a marginal position in that clan if her husband dies and she has no male children (Lind and Eriksen, 2006).

Observations in Kitui suggest that the democratization process that has taken place in Kenya over the past decade may contribute to reducing vulnerability among some poor groups. Increased transfer of development funds from the government to the local level and representation of different clans, including the less wealthy ones, in development committees appears to have led to increased investment in water provision, schools and markets, which are important to the strategies of the poor (as well as the non-poor) to adapting to drought. Nevertheless, in the absence of sufficient social and physical infrastructure and insurance mechanisms, engaging in multiple non-farm livelihood activities has been the main way that households in the area survive crises such as droughts or floods. Such coping strategies include, in addition to assistance from relatives and fellow clan members, local casual employment, migration or relying on remittances, charcoal production, sale of poultry and livestock, production and sale of handicrafts, trading, collection of wild fruit for own consumption and sale, honey production, or collection and sale of firewood and other forest products (Eriksen et al., 2005). Such adaptations, based on multiple activities and diversification of sources of food income and security, have been observed in many areas of Africa (Ellis, 1988; Chambers, 1995). The strategies of the poor to secure material needs are much wider than employment, and include accessing both tangible and intangible assets, such as a diversity of natural resources and social networks (Adams et al., 1998; Carney, 1998; Homewood, 2005).

The availability of such coping strategies is a key facet of adaptive capacity among households. But diversification may also form part of a response to a process of social change and shifting livelihoods, generating increased vulnerability. In the Kitui area, droughts combined with conflicts and insecurity and exclusion from the forest in connection with its gazettement for conservation has led to a loss of livestock for several households, which then had to relocate and resort to cultivation, often on insufficient or marginal lands (Lind and Eriksen 2006). Even on less marginal farmland, it now requires exceptionally favourable rainfall conditions, such as those experienced in some areas in the district in 1997, for households to secure a sufficient income from farming to cover their well-being requirements (Eriksen et al., 2005). There has thus been a general shift from livestock rearing to settled cultivation, while the profitability of farming has also been declining. As a result, there has been an increased need to engage in non-farm activities. But for many, these coping strategies are not sufficient to secure well-being. Only a few households have the labour, skills and capital required to engage in strategies that yield a reliable and viable income, such as skilled employment or larger scale trade. Most households are only able to engage in activities that yield marginal incomes, such as casual employment or collection of forest fruits (Eriksen et al., 2005). The degradation of ecosystem services, as well as loss of access to natural resources through tenure changes, commercialization or creation of nature conservation areas may all contribute to the declining viability of many off-farm livelihood options in several areas in Africa (Reardon and Vosti, 1995; Bowen et al., 2003; Brockington, 2005; Hassan et al., 2005; Eriksen et al., 2006a, 2006b). Moreover, it has been suggested that deagrarianization and diversification, along with declining agricultural performance and profitability, may actually be contributing to marginalization processes and poverty trends in Africa (Bryceson, 1996; Movik et al., 2005; Ellis, 2006; Rigg, 2006). The exclusion of pastoralists from drought watering and grazing areas as well as lack of veterinary and security infrastructure contribute to sedentarization and forms of livelihoods that are less well adapted to a variable climate at the same time as the viability of alternative livelihood options that are accessible to the poor are also declining. The livelihood shifts described above may therefore be undermining the adaptive capacity of poor households in the long run (Eriksen et al., 2006c).

4. Sustainable adaptation measures

The previous discussion has shown that risks posed by, for example, droughts interact closely with the way in which poor households adapt to climate stress, as well as with societal changes, processes and power relations. One implication is that one of the vulnerability–poverty linkages cannot be effectively addressed without at least taking into account the other two linkages in any given vulnerability and poverty context. While it is useful to take into account the physical impacts of climate change in existing programmes and activities, broader considerations of vulnerability to climate change into these activities are necessary if adaptation is to take place in a way that also contributes to poverty reduction.

Table 1 exemplifies sustainable adaptation measures. Risk reduction, for example in the form of improving early warning and evacuation procedures during drought, has been the focus of adaptation efforts by development agencies such as DANIDA and GTZ (Klein et al., 2007). A focus on climate risks to education, health, and social and cultural rights would, in the case of Kitui, imply measures to improve transport and roads, communications and accessibility during floods in order to counteract geographical isolation. Furthermore, adjustments such as timing of the payment of school fees to avoid drought times of the year could help people to benefit from education in the face of climate stress. Physical infrastructure, especially related to water and energy provision, could be made more resilient to climate change. Satisfying energy needs is often difficult because hydroelectric power generation and distribution are affected by both droughts and floods. The use of alternative energy sources such as solar panels, although increasing, is still in its infancy in terms of access by the poor (Venema and Cisse, 2004; Eriksen et al., 2007).

Because the particular risk varies from place to place and between different groups, measures targeted at risks may be very specific to a particular situation; for example, potential reductions in agricultural productivity due to climate stress can be targeted through measures aimed at changing cropping patterns and technologies. In Senegal, pilot farms are adapting to successive droughts and a drier climate by planting dense perennial hedges that act as windbreaks, generating a microclimate conducive to agriculture (Seck et al., 2005). However, one of the main challenges to implementing adaptation interventions aimed at reducing risk (e.g. introducing drought-resistant crops) is that many such measures require skills, capital or labour that poor households do not have. If these measures end up mainly benefiting only a few relatively better-off farmers, such measures may in fact reinforce social differentiation in a village and constitute unsustainable adaptation. Instead, measures that target risks related to climate change combined with measures aimed at strengthening local adaptive capacity may be more effective in reducing vulnerability, as has been attempted in two drought-prone villages in Rajasthan in India (Chatterjee et al., 2005). Some measures, such as improvement of infrastructure and improved techniques of water conservation, can both contribute to reducing risk and to strengthening coping strategies during drought if focused specifically on facilitating the ways in which poor people seek to secure well-being in the face of droughts and floods.

The adaptive capacity linkage between vulnerability and poverty emphasizes the importance of multiactivity and multilocality in the ways in which people seek to secure well-being. An implication is that efforts targeting the sensitivity and performance of just one sector, such as the agricultural sector, are likely to constitute unsustainable adaptations. In order to reduce the vulnerability of the rural poor, measures have to target the multiple sectors and spheres in which people are engaged. In the case of Kitui, securing migration routes for livestock keepers, supporting veterinary, physical and social infrastructure in those areas, and ensuring access rights to important drought grazing areas would enhance adaptation to drought. Strengthening on-farm planting of indigenous trees and improving forest access, in addition to enhancing the processing and value-adding of drought products such as indigenous fruits, gums and resins, could also enhance the viability of forest-based livelihood options (Owuor et al., 2005; Eriksen et al. 2006c). Similarly, Toulmin (2005) argues that enabling movement across national frontiers, installing transparent systems for outsiders to gain access to land, and providing reliable channels for migrants' remittances would enhance mobility and flexibility critical to people's adaptive capacity in the face of climatic variability and change in Africa.

TABLE 1 Potential measures aimed at implementing adaptation in the context of poverty reduction: some examples

	Vulnerability–poverty linkage	Sustainable adaptation measure
Climate risk	Threat to lives and incomes from flood, droughts, heatwaves, cyclones in rural and urban areas	Improving early warning and evacuation procedures
	Agricultural production inhibited by climate variability and change	National agricultural insurance schemes
		Planting of windbreakers
		Diversification of crops
	Melting of glaciers, floods and droughts threatening water supply of the poor	Water conservation, construction of wells
	Energy supply interrupted	Improve local renewable energy options
	Damage to infrastructure and accessibility to social infrastructure	Physical infrastructure and housing made more climate resilient
	Unsanitary conditions during flood and drought and spread of disease	Strengthen health facilities and accessibility to the poor
	Reduced school attendance	Adjust timing of school fee payment
Adaptive capacity	Multiactivity and multilocality	Strengthen multiple economic sectors in which the poor engage
		Enable migration and movement across frontiers
	Migration with cattle to access grazing	Improve services along livestock migration routes
		Ensure rights to drought grazing areas
	Adjustment of crop types	Conservation and research in local strains and crop types
	Social networks and informal income options	Ensure equitable access to key adaptation resources like water
		Investment in and support for local adaptation strategies
	Construction of drought water sources and small scale irrigation	Strengthen on-farm planting of indigenous trees and enhance flexible drought access to forest
	Use of forest products	Improve value adding, processing of local forest products
Processes	Deagrarianization and declining profitability of agriculture	Enhance status and investment in small-scale agriculture
	Marginalization of non-farm incomes	Legalization and regulation of non-farm drought incomes, such as charcoal
		Removing restrictions on the urban informal sector
	Reduced formal employment options	Address unequal resource access structures, barriers of poor to access formal non-farm income opportunities, gender inequality
	Economic globalization	Improved marketing channels and pricing of local products, facilitating local trade
	Spread of HIV/AIDS	Strengthen health and education services, target HIV/AIDS
	Environmental degradation, reinforced by climate change	Mitigation of environmental change
		Enhanced local participation in natural resource management

TABLE 1 Potential measures aimed at implementing adaptation in the context of poverty reduction: some examples *(Cont'd)*

Vulnerability–poverty linkage	Sustainable adaptation measure
Disempowerment	Enhanced democratic participation in development
	Bringing together formal and informal regulatory systems in urban planning
Processes	Strengthen collective management of natural resources important for local adaptation strategies
Conflict and political processes	Strengthen peace committees, civil society and local democratic control over development funds
	Strengthen social welfare programmes for the destitute

(left vertical label: Processes)

The above discussion has showed that the increasing need to diversify into non-farm livelihood options during drought, coupled with the increasing marginality of such livelihoods, can be considered a key cause of vulnerability in some contexts. In such cases, enhancing the urban and rural employment opportunities that could be accessed by vulnerable groups, and reducing barriers to more viable off-farm income sources constitute important adaptation measures. The processes that lead to exclusion from such opportunities, including social marginalization based on gender or ethnicity, as well as entry barriers related to capital, education and skills, could be addressed through such measures. It has been suggested that removing restrictions on the urban informal sector activities could reduce the insecurity, anxiety and humiliation of poor artisans, vendors and entrepreneurs, as well as the petty rents they otherwise have to pay to officials (Chambers, 1995).

Although the case of Kitui has demonstrated several linkages between vulnerability and poverty, the critical lesson is that not all adaptation measures will reduce poverty, nor will all poverty reduction measures represent adaptations to climate change. Returning to our Kenyan example, insecurity and raiding, which had been a feature in the area until the 1990s, has subsided with the advent of peaceful relations, and trade in livestock, food and domestic goods and renting out of wells and grazing lands to pastoralists have since become main sources of income among settled agro-pastoralists in one area of Kitui during drought. In 2006, however, there were attempts by individuals to instigate violence, to exclude pastoralists from the area, and to stop trading activities, possibly due to particular political motives. In addition to such conflict, one of the most important threats to sustainable adaptation was a plan to fence off a large part of the area for commercial ranching, facilitating permanent grazing through water provision within the ranch. While this might reduce poverty among those farmers included in the ranch, it could dramatically increase vulnerability to climate change among most households in the area, since the fences would effectively cut the village off from the plains and wet-season livestock grazing areas on the distant side of the ranch and reinforce shifts from livestock keeping to sedentary farming. It would also prevent trade between nomadic pastoralists from other areas and settled agro-pastoralists. Exclusion from forests due to gazettement for conservation in some areas and privatization of resources in other areas constituted the other major threat to local adaptive capacity. In this case, sustainable adaptation measures would include civil society support such as strengthening collective management of the resources that are important for local coping and adaptive strategies. In addition, an important measure that contributed to sustainable adaptation was the strengthening of a democratically elected peace committee that prevented violence, loss of lives and possessions, and ensured continued trade through 2006 (Eriksen et al., 2006c).

5. Conclusions and implications for sustainable development

The linkages between vulnerability and poverty, and the types of measures that target these linkages, which we refer to as sustainable adaptation measures, have several important implications for development policy and climate change policy. First, a broader set of measures is required than that which has been the focus of adaptation efforts thus far. Adaptation does not entail simply the addition of a scenario of linear changes in average climatic conditions to present activities. Instead, it involves the addition of some consideration of climate change *vulnerability* to present activities. This underscores the suggestion by Schipper and Pelling (2006) that a focus on underlying causes of vulnerability will more effectively facilitate development than a narrow sectoral approach addressing climate change impacts. There are three types of measures that will effectively target this interface:

- those measures that target the risk posed by climate change to the poor, such as the destruction or deterioration of water and social infrastructure and the viability of cropping systems and other sources of livelihoods
- those measures that aim to strengthen the capacity to cope with and adapt to climate stress, such as engaging in alternative sources of income during drought, accessing forest products, or seasonal movements of livestock for grazing
- those measures that address the causes of vulnerability, such as poor market relations in trading in niche drought products, conflict, or poor social and physical infrastructure.

Some of these measures may require a new way of thinking about development and adaptation. Although there is overlap, vulnerability reduction and poverty reduction are not the same thing. Each and every poverty reduction measure does not necessarily contribute to adaptation, and equally – if not more important – each and every climate change vulnerability reduction measure does not automatically contribute to poverty reduction. People's responses to shocks and longer-term changes can be both facilitated and hindered by government policies and measures. For example, migration and mobility are becoming increasingly important for income generation in response to climate change, and policies that tie people to small-scale agriculture and impose other constraints to mobility may in fact generate poverty. As another example, in some areas, local varieties of seeds that are well adapted to local climate conditions are disappearing because of agricultural development projects (Orindi and Ochieng, 2005). In many cases, development is contributing to increased vulnerability through a variety of socio-economic, political, environmental and cultural factors (Yamin et al., 2005).

A second implication is that the mode of implementing measures needs to capture the specificity of each vulnerability context. Because of variations in public policy, aid policy, historical, geographical and other factors, there are substantial differences in vulnerability to climate variability and change across regions and groups. The measures described in this article should be regarded as an exemplification of an approach rather than a prescription. There is an array of possible measures that may contribute to sustainable adaptation, each specific context demanding a different set of measures. It is critical to understand, in any given context, both how people secure or fail to secure the four categories of well-being (material needs, rights, health and basic education, and social and cultural affiliation), the way that climate change poses a risk to people's strategies, the particular ways in which people cope and adapt to climate stress, as well as the main causes or drivers of their vulnerability.

A third implication, given the broad nature of measures required for reduction of vulnerability of the poor, is that adaptation is a social development issue as much as (if not more than) an environmental and technological issue. This means that adaptation to climate change is not simply a local activity, since enhancing empowerment and equity often entails addressing the political and economic structures and frameworks within which people adapt. Since one of the outcomes of vulnerability to climate variability and change is increased poverty, it seems likely that including such sustainable adaptation measures in development can contribute to poverty reduction measures by enhancing people's well-being in the face of climate change. Although climate change seems marginal compared with the pressing issues of poverty reduction, hunger, health, economic development and energy needs, it is becoming increasingly clear that the realization of poverty reduction goals can be seriously hampered by climate change (Schipper and Pelling, 2006).

There are several institutional barriers that may inhibit the adoption of a broader development approach to adaptation (Klein et al., 2007). So far, environment and development have been treated as separate issues within governments, development institutions, and climate change organizations. Adaptation responsibilities are often located within environmental departments as an add-on to the mitigation of greenhouse gas emissions, and hence vulnerability reduction is often treated as an environmental rather than a development problem. Reducing vulnerability also demands measures that are less tangible or clear-cut than traditional environmental measures, and such measures require a higher level of understanding and awareness of vulnerability. It may be for this reason that many initial efforts have focused on reducing biophysical risks. We argue that although such efforts represent a good start, they are not sufficient to achieve sustainable development. Vulnerability and poverty cannot be addressed together unless, in addition to the biophysical risks associated with climate change, the specific risks to the well-being of the poor, their adaptive capacity, and the processes shaping vulnerability are also targeted. Sustainable adaptation measures should contribute positively to one linkage, and at the very least they should not contribute negatively to the other two. However, an integrated combination of adaptation measures is likely to be the most effective in achieving sustainable development in the face of climate change. In particular, the close interaction between the three vulnerability–poverty linkages means that sustainable adaptation measures should treat these as inter-related, rather than as separate spheres for intervention.

Acknowledgements

The authors would like to thank two anonymous reviewers for constructive comments on an earlier draft, as well as Kristian Stokke for help with the figure. Parts of the research reported in this article were initiated in the larger NORAD-funded study 'Climate Change Adaptation and Poverty Reduction: Key Interactions and Critical Measures' to which Richard Klein, Lars Otto Næss and Kirsten Ulsrud also contributed.

References

Adams, A.M., Cekan, J., Sauerborn, R., 1998, 'Towards a conceptual framework of household coping: Reflections from rural West Africa', *Africa* 68, 263–283.
Adato, M., Carter, M.R., May, J., 2006, 'Exploring poverty traps and social exclusion in South Africa using qualitative and quantitative data', *Journal of Development Studies* 42, 226–247.
Adger, W.N., Kelly, P.M., 1999, 'Social vulnerability to climate change and the architecture of entitlements', *Mitigation and Adaptation Strategies for Global Change* 4, 253–266.
Adger, W.N., Hughes, T.P., Folke, C., Carpenter, S., Rockström, J., 2005, 'Social-ecological resilience to coastal disasters', *Science* 309, 1036–1039.

AfDB, ADB, DFID, EC DG Development, BMZ, DGIS, OECD, UNDP, UNEP, World Bank, 2003, *Poverty and Climate Change: Reducing the Vulnerability of the Poor through Adaptation*, World Bank, Washington, DC.

Agrawala, S., 2004, 'Adaptation, development assistance and planning: challenges and opportunities', *IDS Bulletin* 35, 50–54.

Bailis, R., Kirubi, C., Jacobsen, A., 2006, *Sustainable Energy in Kenya*, Policy Brief, ACTS, Nairobi, Kenya.

Bowen, M.L., Chilundo, A., Tique, C.A., 2003, 'Social differentiation, farming practices and environmental change in Mozambique', in: T.J. Bassett, D. Crummey (eds), *African Savannas: Global Narratives and Local Knowledge of Environmental Change*, James Currey, Oxford, UK, 225–247.

Brockington, D., 2005, 'The contingency of community conservation', in: K. Homewood (ed.), *Rural Resources and Local Livelihoods in Africa*, James Currey, Oxford, UK, 100–120.

Bryceson, D.F., 1996, 'Deagrarianization and rural employment in sub-Saharan Africa: a sectoral perspective', *World Development* 24, 97–111.

Burton, I., Huq, S., Lim, B., Pilifosova, O., Schipper, E.L., 2002, 'From impacts assessment to adaptation priorities: the shaping of adaptation policy', *Climate Policy* 2, 145–159.

Carney, D. (ed.), 1998, *Sustainable Rural Livelihoods: What Contributions Can We Make?* Department for International Development, London.

Chambers, R., 1989, 'Vulnerability, coping and policy: introduction', *IDS Bulletin* 20, 1–7.

Chambers, R., 1995, 'Poverty and livelihoods: whose reality counts?' *Environment and Urbanization* 7, 173–204.

Chatterjee, K., Chatterjee, A., Das, S., 2005, 'Community adaptation to drought in Rajasthan', *IDS Bulletin* 36, 33–52.

Christie, F., Hanlon, J., 2001, *Mozambique and the Great Flood of 2000*, James Currey, Oxford, UK.

Christoff, P., 1996, 'Ecological modernisation, ecological modernities', *Environmental Politics* 5, 476–500.

Coetzee, E., 2002, 'Urban vulnerability: a conceptual framework', in: C. Nomdo, E. Coetzee (eds), *Urban Vulnerability. Perspectives from Southern Africa*, Peripheri Publications, Cape Town, 2–27.

Cohen, S., Demeritt, J., Robinson, J., Rothman, D., 1998, 'Climate change and sustainable development: towards dialogue', *Global Environmental Change* 8, 341–371.

Costanza, R., 2003, 'Social goals and the valuation of natural capital', *Environmental Monitoring and Assessment* 86, 19–28.

CPRC (Chronic Poverty Research Centre), 2004, *Chronic Poverty Report 2004-2005*, CPRC, Manchester, UK.

Davies, S., 1993, 'Are coping strategies a cop out?' *IDS Bulletin* 24, 60–72.

Dollar, D., Kraay, A., 2004, 'Trade, growth, and poverty', *Economic Journal* 114(February), F22–F29.

Eakin, H., 2006, *Weathering Risk in Rural Mexico: Climatic, Institutional, and Economic Change*, The University of Arizona Press, Tucson, AZ.

Ellis, F., 1988, 'Household strategies and rural livelihood diversification', *Journal of Development Studies* 35, 1–38.

Ellis, F., 2006, 'Agrarian change and rising vulnerability in rural sub-Saharan Africa', *New Political Economy* 11, 387–397.

Eriksen, S., Brown, K., Kelly, P.M., 2005, 'The dynamics of vulnerability: locating coping strategies in Kenya and Tanzania', *Geographical Journal* 171, 287–305.

Eriksen, S., Gachathi, F.N., Muok, B., Ochieng, B., Owuor, B., 2006a, 'Synergies in biodiversity conservation and climate change adaptation: the case of hilltop forests in Kitui, Kenya', in: J. Mistry J., A. Berardi (eds), *The Savanna Biome System*, Ashgate, Aldershot, UK, 187–226.

Eriksen, S., Owuor, B., Nyukuri, E., Orindi, V. (eds), 2006b, *Vulnerability to Climate Stress – Local and Regional Perspectives: Proceedings of Two Workshops*, CICERO, Oslo.

Eriksen, S., Ulsrud, K., Lind, J., Muok, B., 2006c, *The Urgent Need to Increase Adaptive Capacities*, Policy Brief, ACTS, Nairobi, Kenya.

Eriksen, S.H., Klein, R.J.T., Ulsrud, K., Næss, L.O., O'Brien, K., 2007, *Climate Change Adaptation and Poverty Reduction: Key Interactions and Critical Measures*, GECHS Report 2007:1, University of Oslo, Oslo.

Füssel, H.M., Klein, R.J.T., 2006, 'Climate change vulnerability assessments: an evolution of conceptual thinking', *Climatic Change* 75, 301–329.

Glantz, M., 1994, *Drought Follows the Plow: Cultivating Marginal Areas*, Cambridge University Press, Cambridge, UK.

Handmer, J.W., Dovers, S., Downing, T.E., 1999, 'Societal vulnerability to climate change and variability', *Mitigation and Adaptation Strategies for Global Change* 4, 267–281.

Hassan, R., Scholes, R., Ash, N. (eds), 2005, *Ecosystems and Human Well-being. Volume 1, Current State and Trends: Findings of the Condition and Trends Working Group*, Millennium Ecosystem Assessment, UNEP, Nairobi, Kenya.

Homewood, K., 2005, 'Conclusion: rural resources, local livelihoods and poverty concepts', in: K. Homewood (ed.), *Rural Resources and Local Livelihoods in Africa*, James Currey, Oxford, UK, 198–205.

Kahn, M., 2005, 'The death toll from natural disasters: the role of income, geography, and institutions', *Review of Economics and Statistics* 87, 271–284.

Kelly, P.M., Adger, W.N., 2000, 'Theory and practice in assessing vulnerability to climate change and facilitating adaptation', *Climatic Change* 47, 325–352.

Klein, R.J.T., Eriksen, S., Næss, L.O., Hammill, A., Tanner, T.M., Robledo, C., O'Brien, K., 2007, 'Portfolio screening to support the mainstreaming of adaptation to climate change into development', *Climatic Change* 84, 23–44.

Leichenko R., O'Brien K., 2002, 'The dynamics of rural vulnerability to global change', *Mitigation and Adaptation Strategies for Global Change*, 7, 1–18.

Lind, J., Eriksen, S., 2006, 'The impacts of conflict on household coping strategies: evidence from Turkana and Kitui Districts in Kenya', *Die Erde* 137, 249–270.

Markandya, A., Halsnæs, K., 2002, *Climate Change and Sustainable Development: Prospects for Developing Countries*, Earthscan, London.

Movik, S., Mehta, L., Mitsi, S., Nicol, A., 2005, 'A "blue revolution" for African agriculture?' *IDS Bulletin* 36, 41–45.

O'Brien, G., O'Keefe, P., Rose, J., Wisner, B., 2006, 'Climate change and disaster management', *Disasters* 30, 64–80.

O'Brien K., Eriksen, S., Nygaard, L., Schjolden, A., 2007, 'Why different interpretations of vulnerability matter in climate change discourses', *Climate Policy* 7, 73–88.

OECD, 2001, *The DAC Guidelines Poverty Reduction*, Organisation for Economic Co-operation and Development, Paris.

Orindi, V., Ochieng, A., 2005, 'Case study 5: Kenya – seed fairs as a drought recovery strategy in Kenya', *IDS Bulletin* 36, 87–102.

Owuor, B., Eriksen, S., Mauta, W., 2005, 'Adapting to climate change in a dryland mountain environment in Kenya', *Mountain Research and Development* 25, 310–315.

Øyen, E., 2005, *The Poliscopic Landscape of Poverty Research: "State of the Art" in International Poverty Research – An Overview and 6 In-depth Studies*, CROP, Bergen, Norway.

Parry, M.L., Canziani, O.F., Palutikof, J.P., van der Linden, P.J., Hanson, C.E. (eds), 2007, *Climate Change 2007: Impacts, Adaptation and Vulnerability. Contribution of Working Group II to the Fourth Assessment Report of the Intergovernmental Panel on Climate Change*, Cambridge University Press, Cambridge, UK.

Reardon, T., Vosti, S., 1995, 'Links between rural poverty and the environment in developing countries: asset categories and investment poverty', *World Development* 23, 1495–1506.

Rigg, J., 2006, 'Land, farming, livelihoods, and poverty: rethinking the links in the rural South', *World Development* 34, 180–202.

Sachs, J., 2005, *The End of Poverty: Economic Possibilities for our Time*, Penguin Press, New York.

Schipper, L., Pelling, M., 2006, 'Disaster risk, climate change and international development: scope for, and challenges to, integration', *Disasters* 30, 19–38.

Scoones, I., Chibudu, C., Chikura, S., Jeranyama, P., Machaka, D., Machanja, W., Mavedzenge, B., Mombeshora, B., Mudhara, M., Mudziwo, C., Murimbarimba, F., Zirereza, B., 1996, *Hazard and Opportunities: Farming Livelihoods in Dryland Africa – Lessons from Zimbabwe*, Zed Books and International Institute for Environment and Development, London.

Seck, M., Abou Mamouda, M.N., Wade, S., 2005, 'Case study 4: Senegal – adaptation and mitigation through "produced environments": the case for agriculture intensification in Senegal', *IDS Bulletin* 36, 71–86.

Sen, A.K., 1981, *Poverty and Famines: An Essay on Entitlement and Deprivation*, Clarendon Press, Oxford, UK.

Sen, A., 1999, *Development as Freedom*, Anchor Books, New York.

Smit, B., Pilifosova, O., 2001, 'Adaptation to climate change in the context of sustainable development and equity', in: J.J. McCarthy, O.F. Canziani, N.A. Leary, D.J. Dokken, K.S. White (eds), *Climate Change 2001: Impacts, Adaptation, and Vulnerability*, Cambridge University Press, Cambridge, UK, 877–912.

Swart, R., Robinson, J., Cohen, S., 2003, 'Climate change and sustainable development: expanding the options', *Climate Policy* 3(S1), S19–S40.

Thomalla, F., Downing, T., Spanger-Siegfried, E., Han, G., Rockström, J., 2006, 'Reducing hazard vulnerability: towards a common approach between disaster risk reduction and climate adaptation', *Disasters* 30, 39–48.

Thomas, D.S.G., Twyman, C., 2005, 'Equity and justice in climate change adaptation amongst natural-resource-dependent societies', *Global Environmental Change* 15, 115–124.

Tol, R.S.J., Downing, T.E., Kuik, O.J., Smith, J.B., 2004, 'Distributional aspects of climate change impacts', *Global Environmental Change* 14, 259–272.

Toulmin, C., 2005, *Africa: Make Climate Change History*, openDemocracy [available at www.openDemocracy.net].

UNEP/IISD, 2004, *Exploring the Links: Human Well-Being, Poverty and Ecosystem Services*, UNEP/IISD, Nairobi, Kenya, and Winnipeg, Manitoba, Canada.

Venema, H.D., Cisse, M. (eds), 2004, *Seeing the Light: Adapting to Climate Change with Decentralized Renewable Energy in Developing Countries*, Climate Change Knowledge Network and International Institute for Sustainable Development, Canada.

Watson, H.K., 2002, 'The sustainability of southern Africa's savanna resources', in: H. Baijnath, Y. Singh (eds), *A Rebirth of Science in Africa: A Vision for Life and Environmental Sciences*, UMDAS Press, Pretoria, South Africa, 160–174.

Wisner, B., Blaikie, P., Cannon, T., Davis, I., 2004, *At Risk: Natural Hazards, People's Vulnerability and Disasters*, Routledge, UK.

Wood, G., 2003, 'Staying secure, staying poor: the "Faustian bargain"', *World Development* 31, 455–471.

Yamin, F., Rahman, A., Huq, S., 2005, 'Vulnerability, adaptation and climate disasters: a conceptual overview', *IDS Bulletin* 36, 1–14.

Yohe, G.W., Lasco, R.D., Ahmad, Q.K., Arnell, N.W., Cohen, S.J., Hope, C., Janetos, A.C., Perez, R.T., 2007, 'Perspectives on climate change and sustainability', in: M.L. Parry, O.F. Canziani, J.P. Palutikof, P.J. van der Linden, C.E. Hanson (eds), *Climate Change 2007: Impacts, Adaptation and Vulnerability. Contribution of Working Group II to the Fourth Assessment Report of the Intergovernmental Panel on Climate Change*, Cambridge University Press, Cambridge, UK, 811–841.

Ziervogel, G., Bharwani, S., Downing, T.E., 2006, 'Adapting to climate variability: pumpkins, people and policy', *Natural Resources Forum* 30, 294–305.

■ synthesis article

Structured decision-making to link climate change and sustainable development

CHARLIE WILSON, TIM MCDANIELS*

Institute for Resources, Environment and Sustainability, University of British Columbia, Vancouver, Canada

Structured decision-making concepts and tools have been broadly applied in a wide range of policy contexts to help advance clear, creative and pluralistic decision processes. Policies to link climate change adaptation and mitigation with sustainable development must address a number of complexities which include linkages across scales and irreducible uncertainties. Decision support tools such as objectives networks and influence diagrams are useful for structuring these complex decision problems. These tools and their underlying rationale are described, and then applied to a concrete example to illustrate their relevance for linking adaptation, mitigation and sustainable development decisions. The example used is a major transportation infrastructure programme in British Columbia, Canada, with clear impacts on both climate change and regional sustainability.

Keywords: climate change; decision support tools; governance; integrated policy; stakeholder participation; structured decision-making; sustainable development; transport planning

Les concepts et outils servant à structurer la prise de décision ont été largement appliqués dans une multitude de contextes politiques en vue d'améliorer la clarté, la créativité et la pluralité des procédés décisionnels. Les politiques visant à lier changement climatique (mitigation et adaptation) au développement durable, doivent incorporer un certain nombre de questions complexes y compris les liens à travers différences d'échelles et les incertitudes irréductibles. Les instruments d'aide à la décision, tels que les réseaux d'objectifs et les diagrammes d'influence peuvent aider à structurer ces problèmes de prise de décision complexes. Ces instruments et leur logique sous-jacente sont décrits puis appliqués dans le contexte d'un exemple concret, en vue de démontrer leur intérêt pour lier les décisions sur l'adaptation, la mitigation et le développement durable. L'exemple employé est celui d'un grand programme d'infrastructure de transport en Colombie-Britannique(Canada), où les impacts en matière de changement climatique et développement local sont clairs.

Mots clés: changement climatique; développement durable; gouvernance; instruments d'aide à la décision; planification transport; participation publique; politique intégrée; prise de décision structurée

1. Introduction

Responding to climate change will require complex decisions by individuals, organizations and governments for the foreseeable future (IPCC, 2001).[1] A recent theme in the writing on *adaptation* and *mitigation* (AM) stresses the potential gains that can occur from recognizing that decisions to address either of these contexts may have implications for the other context.[2] A still broader viewpoint from which to consider the impacts of mitigation or adaptation actions is how they may affect the aggregate *sustainable development* (SD) of a region or community (see other articles in this special issue).

■ *Corresponding author. E-mail*: timmcd@interchange.ubc.ca

CLIMATE POLICY 7 (2007) 353–370

© 2007 Earthscan ISSN: 1469-3062 (print), 1752-7457 (online) www.climatepolicy.com

The underlying reasons for considering these linkages among AM and SD decisions can be succinctly stated as follows:

- Many dimensions of the *values* that serve as the motivation for these decisions are, in broad terms, common to all three decision contexts (A, M and SD: hence AMSD). Values can be understood here simply to mean what is ultimately important to decision-makers.
- The impacts from any one of these three decision contexts may have important *consequences* for the other contexts.
- The *choice among alternatives* in one context is therefore a potential means to achieving the underlying values important in the other contexts.

Values, consequences and choices among alternatives are all crucial considerations within the process of decision-making. This article assumes that how AMSD decision processes are structured and communicated to others will have a major influence on the choices made, their acceptability, and thus the progress made toward underlying societal values. It argues that some basic concepts and tools of applied decision-analytic practice, which we refer to as *structured decision-making*, provide insightful ways to help address complexity in these decisions, and also to explicitly link their AM and SD implications. Emphasis is placed on the role of two problem-structuring tools, *objectives hierarchies* (and *means–ends networks*) and *influence diagrams*, as heuristic approaches for exploring and communicating the linkages in AMSD problems. Understanding these linkages is crucial for informed decisions that bridge these diverse contexts.

AMSD decisions share certain characteristics that should be addressed by structured decision processes. First, AMSD decisions often involve multiple scales of impact (across both time and space), and multiple scales of governance (McDaniels et al., 2005; Cash et al., 2006). A second, and related, point is that AMSD decisions involve complex relationships between ends and means: ends (or fundamental objectives) in one context (A or M) may be means in another, broader context (SD). A third major commonality includes uncertainties and path dependence (Arthur, 1994) within AMSD decision contexts, which suggests that approaches are needed to foster learning over time about these repeated decisions. Finally, AMSD decisions would typically be made within pluralistic decision processes, often involving civil society.[3] Hence, clarity regarding the information base and how the decision is structured, as well as transparency and the degree to which the choices are understandable to those involved, will be important aspects for supporting decision-making and the acceptability of decision outcomes.

This article addresses these four commonalities of AMSD decisions through the discussion of concepts, methods and tools, and their stepwise application as a concrete example. The objectives of this article are twofold: firstly, to show how structured decision-making (decision analysis applied in the public domain) can contribute to linking AM and SD in a clear and transparent way; and secondly, to illustrate the specific application of structured decision-making tools.

Section 2 discusses key concepts and practice, focusing on two tools drawn from decision-analytic practice that are highly useful in structuring linkages in complex decisions: objectives networks and influence diagrams. Section 3 applies these tools through a worked example: the Gateway Programme is a major transportation infrastructure development in the Greater Vancouver region of British Columbia, Canada. Section 4 discusses implementation issues with structured decision-making in applied contexts, using examples from the British Columbia natural resource sector. Section 5 concludes by drawing together the practical points made and their applicability to multi-stakeholder decision processes.

2. Structured decision-making: concepts, methods and tools

2.1. Concepts

Decision analysis has developed over the last 50 years as an applied practice founded on subjective expected utility theory for decision-making under uncertainty (Keeney and Raiffa, 1993; Clemen and Reilly, 2001). In recent decades, applied researchers have placed increasing emphasis on the role of a clear decision process in which two fundamental kinds of information are integrated: value-based information (discourse concerned with the underlying values that motivate concern for the decision); and technically based information (judgements regarding potential alternatives and their consequences). Decision analysis combines the two in order to gain insights regarding choice among the alternatives in a given decision context.[4] The components of a well-structured decision process are drawn from the information needs of decision theory, and are similar to the basic steps of policy analysis and planning (e.g. MacRae and Whittington, 1997). These steps have been articulated by many writers (e.g. Dawes, 1988; Hammond et al., 1999; Bazerman, 2001). They involve (1) selecting the decision to be made (defining the problem), (2) clarifying objectives based on the underlying values of decision-makers and interested parties, (3) creating attractive alternatives to achieve the objectives in the context of the problem, (4) examining the consequences of the alternatives, using performance measures in terms of the achievement of objectives, and the uncertainties in those consequences, and (5) exploring the tradeoffs inherent in choosing between the alternatives.[5] In practice, these steps are best considered iteratively, with revision and refinement sufficient to provide an appropriate model that yields sufficient insight for selecting from the alternatives (Phillips, 1984).

Structured decision-making is a 'participant-friendly' term referring to the practice of decision analysis in public policy contexts.[6] This often involves stakeholders in civil society processes that employ both analysis and discourse (Arvai et al., 2001; Renn, 2003). The emphasis on conducting decision processes either in combination with – or subject to the review of – stakeholder processes, places emphasis on the need for clarity, simplicity and effective communication. The information base, judgements and decision process need to be understood by a wide array of interested parties. It also places emphasis on the role of multiple perspectives on values, and multiple perspectives on technical judgements, as a basis for creating more attractive alternatives, and understanding the implications of diverse views.

2.2. Applicability to AMSD

Decision-analytic concepts and methods have been suggested for decisions regarding climate change adaptation and mitigation. Decision theory has been discussed in the IPCC assessment reports as conceptually and practically relevant for understanding both mitigation and adaptation choices (see IPCC, 2001). The UK Climate Impacts Programme (CIP) emphasizes decision-analytic approaches for decision-making under uncertainty as the underlying basis for adaptation decisions (Willows and Connell, 2003). Yet the requirements of the process outlined in the UK CIP document are daunting in practical terms, and published applications are exceedingly rare (UK CIP, 2006). Nor does the guide explicitly discuss issues of linking adaptation decisions to mitigation, nor to the broader perspective of sustainable development. Issues concerning the implementation of structured decision processes in relation to AMSD are further discussed in Section 4.

While an ideal analysis of an AMSD decision would involve all the steps of structured decision-making along with stakeholder involvement, several applications have demonstrated the potential benefits of an analysis that addresses only parts of such a process. For example, Keeney (1992) stressed the crucial role of structuring values from diverse perspectives (value-focused thinking) to serve as the basis for creating more attractive alternatives, identifying information requirements, and conducting evaluation. This one component of the overall decision-analytic structure – clarifying values in terms of objectives and then performance measures – has been shown in many applications to be an important means to achieving better structured decision problems, and thus better decisions (e.g. Keeney and McDaniels, 1999; Clemen and Reilly 2001; Gregory and Keeney, 2002).

2.3. Methods and tools

Section 1 introduced several characteristics of AMSD decisions that should be addressed in order to engender more informed and better structured decision-making. One aspect included *linkages between ends and means* in decision-making, recognizing that these may also involve efforts to *link decisions across multiple scales of governance and impact* (sometimes from local to global) and *across timescales*. A second set included *characterizing uncertainties and opportunities for learning over time*, which also hinges in part on explicit attention to decision contexts. Below we discuss analytical methods for addressing these characteristics of AMSD decisions, and describe two specific structured decision-making tools with examples of how they have been applied.

2.3.1. Methods: structuring objectives

Structured decision-making requires a defined decision context in terms of scope, timescale, policy domain, physical scale and so on. Once the decision context is bounded, structured decision-making emphasizes the use of values (what is important) to specify the fundamental objectives for the decision. These ends can typically be achieved by different means. Several sources discuss the elicitation of objectives important for a decision, based on the expressed viewpoints of interested parties, in order to provide a more complete and informed perspective on what is important to achieve in a decision (e.g. McDaniels, 2000). The distinction between – and linkages among – ends and means can be unravelled through discussion and introspection about the reasons why a given objective is important for that decision (either as a means to addressing another concern or as a fundamental concern motivating interest in the decision) (Keeney, 1992; Clemen and Reilly, 2001). This structuring of the objectives is necessary as they have different analytical functions. Fundamental objectives embody values and are used to derive performance measures for assessing different alternatives. Means objectives outline the consequence pathways that lead from alternatives to outcomes of interest, and are also used to foster creativity in generating alternatives (Keeney, 1992).

Sustainability-related decisions inevitably involve balancing long-term economic, social and environmental well-being as fundamental objectives (McDaniels, 1994). While discussing these objectives in broad terms is commonplace, a more difficult task is to define performance measures that are meaningful and informative for the decision context at hand (Keeney and Gregory, 2005) and relevant for the institutional scale (McDaniels et al., 2005).

2.3.2. Tools: objectives hierarchies and means–ends networks

Keeney (1992) introduced network diagrams to graphically indicate links among the *means* available in a decision context and the ultimate *ends* of importance. An example is shown in Figure 1, taken from the Georgia Basin Futures Project, a 5-year research initiative to explore stakeholders' perspectives on sustainability in the bioregion centred on Vancouver in British Columbia, Canada (Tansey et al., 2002; Robinson, 2003; Carmichael et al., 2004). Part of the research involved 'backcasting'

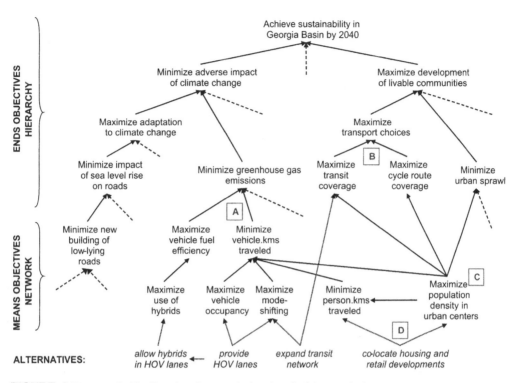

FIGURE 1 Structured objectives in a transport planning decision context.

workshops in which municipal decision-makers devised trajectories to reach their visions of a desirable future. Structured decision-making tools were then used to help create and organize specific policy interventions or 'alternatives' (Wilson and Tansey, 2006). While the broad *strategic* objective for the Georgia Basin Futures Project was sustainability in the bioregion, the example described here and in Figure 1 uses the *specific* decision context of personal transportation incorporating AMSD objectives.

The objectives summarized in Figure 1 were developed from both policy documents and discussions with technical experts and stakeholders in the workshops. The objectives were then structured as follows. First, objective statements that were overlapping or alternate expressions of the same goal were clustered into a single objective. Second, fundamental or ends objectives were distinguished from means objectives using the heuristic that a means objective contributes towards the fundamental objective, which is the ultimate expression of what is important. As an example, a stakeholder might express that 'people should use their cars less'. This value is structured as the objective 'minimize vehicle.km travelled', which is a means towards minimizing greenhouse gas emissions from car use (see box A in Figure 1). Third, the fundamental objectives were structured into a hierarchy. More general objectives at the top of the hierarchy were broken down into lower-level objectives, which can be used to derive performance measures. 'Maximize transport choices' might be disaggregated into 'maximize transit coverage' and 'maximize cycle route coverage' (see box B in Figure 1), with associated performance measures of '% of population within 100 m of transit station/cycle route' respectively. Finally, the means objectives are structured into a network. Unlike the fundamental objectives, a single means objective can impact various other objectives. 'Maximize population density in urban areas' contributes directly to the lower-level fundamental objectives 'minimize urban sprawl' and 'maximize transit coverage', but is also connected to other means objectives including 'minimize person.km travelled' (see box C in Figure 1).

Connections within the means–ends network show the *consequence pathways* (i.e. the sequence of means) by which different alternatives affect the fundamental objectives. These network connections can be further developed: by inserting intermediate objectives as pre-requisites to the fundamental objectives; by further disaggregating objectives; or by expanding the network 'downwards' towards specific policy alternatives.

The network also reveals the interlinkages between the different consequence pathways of an alternative (Clemen and Reilly, 2001). From Figure 1, for example, 'co-locate housing and retail developments' through land-use zoning and planning guidelines is an example of an alternative that would affect the fundamental objectives along various consequence pathways (see box D in Figure 1).

Taken together, the objectives hierarchy and means–ends network define both the fundamental goals for the pluralistic decision process and the means of achieving those goals. The process of structuring objectives requires thought and effort (see Section 4), but is crucial for a clear understanding of the interactions between means objectives, and the tradeoffs to be considered for alternatives that act along different consequence pathways. This enables the sequencing of objectives over time and the linking of objectives across spatial and institutional scales. These linkages are discussed further in Section 3 and also in recent work using objectives networks. For example, McDaniels et al. (2005) discuss the ideal characteristics for governance across multiple scales, and show how constraints defined at one scale require effective governance in terms of competence and legitimacy to be workable and acceptable at another scale. McDaniels et al. (2006) link means–ends networks for regulatory decisions by different institutions to build a risk management framework for salmon aquaculture that crosses multiple scales of governance.

2.3.3. Methods: characterizing relationships and uncertainties

Consequence pathways link alternatives to the fundamental objectives for the decision. While means objectives show the intermediate consequences of interest and how they are interlinked, there are a host of other factors relevant to the decision structure including uncertainties in the probability and magnitude of events, uncertainties in functional relationships, the outcome and nature of known events, the impact of other decisions, and so on. Moreover, many uncertainties in AMSD decisions will be irreducible insofar as they cannot be resolved by further analysis prior to the decision. This requires flexible alternatives that can be modified in response to both exogenous change and endogenous experience. Management strategies that can adapt to learning on how alternatives actually perform against stated objectives are particularly important for long-term, large-scale issues (Dietz et al., 2003). Such strategies, incorporating hypothesis-driven experimentation and explicit learning goals, emerged originally in ecosystem management but are readily applicable in the AMSD domain (Holling, 1978; Arvai et al., 2006). This *in vivo* experience links alternatives to their outcomes, and allows for iterative improvement based on improved understanding. Conversely, alternatives that implicitly or explicitly constrain future choice create problems of path dependency or lock-in (Ruth, 2005).

Influence diagrams are a useful tool in both these regards as they can be used to: (1) represent all the different elements relevant to a decision; (2) show the uncertainties in consequence pathways when designing alternatives; and thus (3) help identify where learning objectives may be most relevant (i.e. where desired outcomes are most contingent). Once experience is gained (and learning objectives met), parts of the influence diagram may then be simplified or collapsed as uncertainties are resolved into known outcomes or parameterized functions.

2.3.4. Tools: influence diagrams

Influence diagrams are a problem-structuring and model-building approach developed in the decision sciences (Howard and Matheson, 1984). They represent the different elements that comprise a decision and show their interrelationships. Different shaped nodes are used to represent decisions, uncertainties, known events or contingent functions (if A then B), and final consequences (see the key to Figure 2). Connecting arrows between the nodes show how one decision element influences or is relevant to another element.

Influence diagrams can have diverse uses in characterizing: probabilistic dependence among variables (Shachter, 1986); 'knowledge maps' (an individual's or group's mental representation of an uncertain variable) (Howard, 1989); different mental models of specific kinds of decisions held by lay people and experts (Morgan et al., 2002); means–ends objectives networks (Keeney, 1992); and complex models, both on paper (Fischhoff, 2006) or using computers (Morgan and Dowlatabadi, 1993). Influence diagrams can also serve as the basis for evaluating decision alternatives in a manner that is formally similar to decision trees (Clemen and Reilly, 2001). The visual characterization of relationships among variables is also a powerful communication device to foster understanding among interested parties in a vast array of contexts.

An example of an influence diagram is given in Figure 2, taken from a study of private property developers' decisions to connect to a district energy system in Vancouver, British Columbia (Wilson et al., 2006). Decentralized energy technologies and systems are often cited as a 'no-regrets' AM intervention with ancillary non-climate (or SD) benefits to further justify their implementation

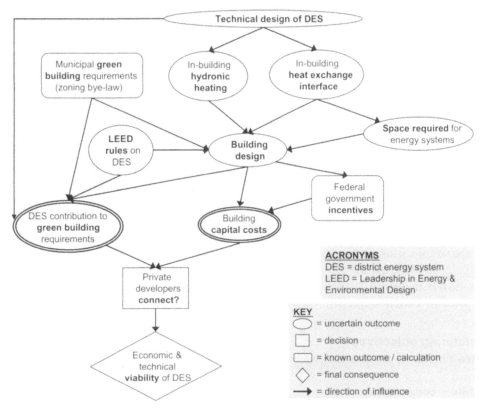

FIGURE 2 A developer's decision to connect to a district energy system (DES).

(IPCC, 2001; Ruth, 2005). The influence diagram shows the key information that is relevant to the decision (the rectangular-shaped decision node near the bottom: 'private developers connect?').

To be viable economically, the district energy system ('DES' in Figure 2) needed sufficient numbers of developers to connect their buildings (the diamond-shaped final consequence node at the bottom: 'economic and technical viability of DES'). As a result, the municipal sponsor of the system was interested in the influences on developers' decisions so that it could potentially introduce new decision elements or change existing ones to facilitate developers' decisions to connect. The two main uncertainties or unresolved outcomes of direct influence are represented by the oval-shaped uncertainty nodes: 'DES contribution to green building requirements' and 'building capital costs'. A network of influences links these uncertainties back up to the 'technical design of DES' (the uncertainty node at the top) whose details were not fully certain when the decisions were taken.

While useful in isolation, influence diagrams can also be linked into the hierarchy of fundamental objectives to help analyse how different decision elements influence the desired consequences (see Section 3).[7]

3. Applying structured decision-making to an AMSD problem

3.1. The Gateway Programme

The Gateway Programme is a multi-billion dollar expansion of the arterial road network for the Greater Vancouver region in the province of British Columbia, Canada (BC Ministry of Transportation, 2006a).[8] Substantial new road and bridge infrastructure is slated for construction in 2007–2012 to relieve congestion on major commercial transportation and commuter routes. Congestion management measures such as tolling and high-occupancy vehicle ('HOV') lanes are also being considered. The Gateway Programme is designed to complement ongoing improvements to the regional road and transit network. Some stakeholders have criticized the Gateway Programme for its potentially perverse impact on overall traffic volumes (MacPhee et al., 2006; Montgomery, 2006; Doherty, 2007).

According to provincial government documents (BC Ministry of Transportation, 2006a), the Gateway Programme's ultimate goals are to promote quality of life and economic growth, both common features of sustainable development policies. However, despite the importance of transport infrastructure to both adaptation and mitigation objectives, the planning framework for the Gateway Programme lacks any explicit consideration of climate change. As a public policy decision, the Gateway Programme also lacks clearly structured objectives and an evaluation of competing alternatives against those objectives.

This makes the Gateway Programme a useful counterfactual example of how structured decision-making *could* be used to link climate change and sustainable development in a comprehensive and transparent decision process. Here we work stepwise through the concepts and tools introduced in Section 2 to demonstrate the relevance and applicability of structured decision-making for complex AMSD decisions. Issues concerning how and why structured decision-making may be implemented in contexts like the Gateway Programme are discussed further in Section 4.

3.2. Structuring objectives

The stated objectives for the Gateway Programme are (BC Ministry of Transportation, 2006a):

- to address congestion
- to improve the mobility of goods and people in and through the region

- to improve access to key economic gateways (ports, airports, etc.)
- to improve the road connections between municipalities
- to improve quality of life by removing regional traffic from local streets
- to reduce vehicle emissions by reducing congestion-related idling
- to improve connections to transit, cycling and pedestrian networks
- to reduce travel times (especially during peak periods).

In the absence of any integration or structuring, the relative priorities or weightings for these different objectives cannot be deduced. Furthermore, the extent to which the Gateway Programme as the selected alternative performs against these different objectives is set out only in aggregate terms. No competing alternatives are explicitly presented. In this regard, the Gateway Programme appears to be a prime example of constrained 'alternatives-focused thinking' (Keeney, 1992). In contrast, structured decision-making is founded on clearly articulated objectives as a framework for the creation and assessment of alternatives.

As discussed in Section 2, the first step is to distinguish fundamental from means objectives, organizing the former into a hierarchy and the latter into a network. This structuring process for the list of stated objectives for the Gateway Programme is illustrated in Figure 3. As the Gateway Programme is already selected as the preferred strategy (set of alternatives), it is included in italics at the bottom of Figure 3.

The two fundamental objectives address people and goods, respectively: 'increase quality of life', which is broken down into five lower-level objectives ('transport choices', 'pollution', 'safety',

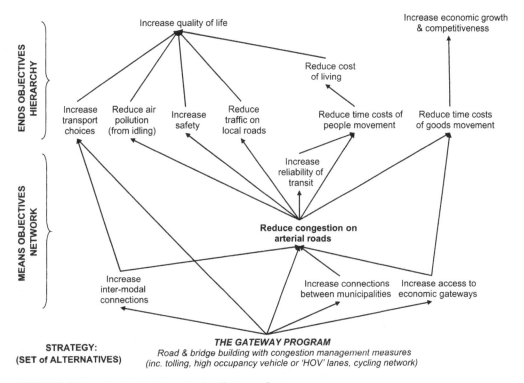

FIGURE 3 Structured objectives for the Gateway Programme.

'local traffic' and 'time costs'); and 'increase economic growth', which is specified further as 'reduce time costs of goods movement'.

'Reducing congestion' is the emphasized objective in the Gateway Programme documentation (shown in bold in Figure 3). However, when all the stated objectives are appropriately structured, it is clear that this is a means rather than an end. One obvious implication is that alternatives to road and bridge building, while not necessarily addressing congestion, may help to achieve the fundamental objectives. Nevertheless, examining the consequence pathways through the means–ends network clearly shows that addressing congestion is the pivotal means objective on which the success of the Gateway Programme depends. This reinforces the importance of congestion management measures as an essential part of the overall strategy.

3.3. Linking objectives among A, M and SD

Structured objectives share a common, consistent and transparent format. This aids AMSD decisions by allowing for climate change objectives to be readily linked to sustainable development objectives for decisions in a specific context. Figures 1 and 3 both concern transportation decisions, and provide a useful example of how this linking can occur. The lower-level fundamental objectives in Figure 1 concern *adaptation* to the impact of sea-level rise on road infrastructure and *mitigation* of greenhouse gas emissions from transport. (These are examples only and are not intended to be exhaustive.) Together with the relevant elements in the means objective network, these can be linked into the existing Gateway Programme objectives in Figure 3 to provide an integrated AMSD decision framework.

This new framework helps stimulate the creation of alternatives that take a broadened range of objectives into account. For example, the 'minimize vehicle.km travelled' objective from Figure 1 might result in strategies to manage the factors driving the demand for mobility in the region as well as, or instead of, the Gateway Programme's focus on new infrastructure. Adaptation objectives might suggest alternatives to road expansion on low-lying deltas and flood plains (both of which are included in the Gateway Programme), or to provide for sea surge protection (dykes, natural barriers).

3.4. Linking across spatial and governance scales

AMSD problems are often relevant to multiple decision-making agencies. Structured decision-making experience shows clearly how fundamental objectives – statements of what is important to the decision-makers – are often widely shared (Gregory and Keeney, 1994; Hobbs and Horne, 1997). Differences in both perspective and purview tend to arise more over preferences for different consequence pathways or means objectives, as these are framed by the regulatory scope of a decision-making agency. However, structured objectives can be readily interlinked to identify overlaps between the domains or competencies of different agencies, as well as the specific areas in which they need to act in concert to achieve shared objectives. The assessment of alternatives helps disentangle common disagreements over facts (e.g. the consequence of an alternative on a given objective) from rarer disagreements over values (e.g. the inclusion and relative weighting of different objectives).

In the case of the Gateway Programme, standardized decision frameworks (e.g. Figures 1 and 3) could facilitate two key interlinkages. The first interlinkage is between regulatory agencies at the provincial scale to integrate climate change objectives (Ministry of Environment) with mobility objectives (Ministry of Transportation). The second interlinkage is across governance scales between the provincial government and the municipalities managing local mobility and land use. The interlinking process is much the same as described above for integrating AM and SD. In this case, the fundamental objectives for different regulatory bodies at different scales would be overlaid, and the subordinate networks of means objectives integrated.[9] With duplications removed, new connections between means and ends in the integrated decision framework would suggest new consequence pathways along which alternatives might act. Further information can be included by assigning each linkage a positive (+), negative (?) or contingent (+/?) direction of influence, as a first step in the assessment of impacts.

In the Gateway Programme, tradeoffs between spatial scales are manifest in the potential impact of the road infrastructure (regional) on land-use planning and development (municipal) (BC Ministry of Transportation, 2006b). The impacts might lead the provincial government to include mitigating measures for municipalities as part of its transportation strategy; for example, additional resources to support municipal zoning, or a land-use planner as part of the project team to work with municipalities.

3.5. Linkages across timescales

In addition to linking across governance and spatial scales, it is common to find different timescales embedded within a single set of structured objectives. The avoidance of specific target or threshold levels in performance criteria make the achievement of fundamental objectives an incremental and dynamic process.[10] However, the timescales over which different alternatives are expected to act allow the means objectives network to be sequenced. From Figure 3, for example, increasing

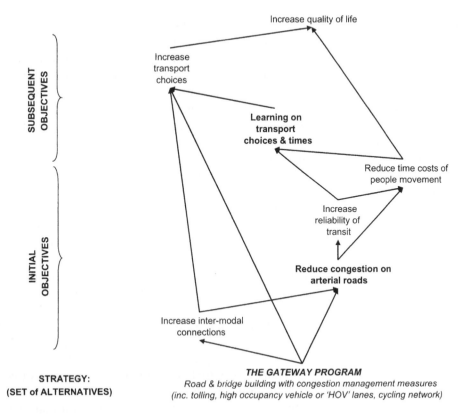

FIGURE 4 Time sequenced objectives.

'inter-modal connections' might affect 'transport choices' only after immediate improvements in 'reliability of transit' are achieved through 'reducing congestion'. While transit reliability and the resulting 'reduced time costs of people movement' might be expected to be immediate consequences of the Gateway Programme, the increase in transport choices as perceived by the travelling public may only be a learning response from personal experience as well as information provided about these reduced time costs. The structured objectives can be modified therefore to distinguish the initial from subsequent (and therefore, contingent) objectives, as shown in Figure 4. Sequencing the timescales embedded within structured objectives often helps reveal these essential intermediate learning stages (McDaniels and Gregory, 2004). Sequencing objectives also helps develop the expected consequence pathways of alternatives. These pathways are primarily causal, but can also include influence diagrams so that key uncertainties and decisions are included (see below for an example).

An alternative to this type of time sequencing is to include proxies for longer-term objectives whose achievements are contingent on more immediate objectives being met. In a climate change context, for example, this would involve near-term objectives for both adaptation and mitigation alongside objectives which characterize an improved capacity or ability to address adaptation and mitigation in the future (Keeney and McDaniels, 2001). This avoids biasing the selection of alternatives towards those that provide immediate gains. Indeed, an important lesson of successful and adaptive management strategies is the importance of avoiding low-probability but high-consequence outcomes in the long term, even though immediate outcomes may be suboptimal (Gunderson and Holling, 2002).

3.6. Managing uncertainties through learning objectives

The key uncertainties in the Gateway Programme concern the behavioural response of vehicle users. Reduced congestion as a consequence of the road and bridge building strategy depends on the effectiveness of congestion management measures (e.g. tolling or HOV lanes), overall demand for mobility, and the uptake of mode switching (see Figures 1 and 3). Explicitly including learning objectives (see Figure 4) would provide for an initial phase of the Gateway Programme, perhaps geographically localized, to help parameterize these uncertainties, and so allow greater confidence in longer-term expected outcomes. Should the forecasts of outcomes no longer reflect the stated objectives, components of the strategy could be modified.

Figure 5 integrates the SD objectives for the Gateway Programme (Figure 3) with the AM objectives from the earlier study of personal transportation in the Greater Vancouver region (left-side of Figure 1). Figure 5 takes the form of an influence diagram which characterizes the key uncertainties mediating the outcomes of the Gateway Programme (as the selected alternative) on the stated objectives. These uncertainties and other influences are based on Gateway Programme documentation.

The top third of Figure 5 shows the fundamental objectives as calculation nodes (rounded rectangles), leading to the final consequences (diamond nodes). A calculation node is a decision element whose outcome can be resolved when the influences on it become known. The AM objectives are on the left, the SD objectives on the right. The middle third of Figure 5 shows how the Gateway Programme's fundamental objectives are contingent on three key uncertainties: 'modal choices and switching', 'movement of people', and 'movement of goods'. These latter two comprise the overall demand for transport, which is a function of socio-demographic and other trends (according to Gateway Programme documentation). These are represented in the calculation nodes in the bottom right of Figure 5. 'Change in socio-demographics' refers to: increased car ownership per capita; households with two working adults (and working children)

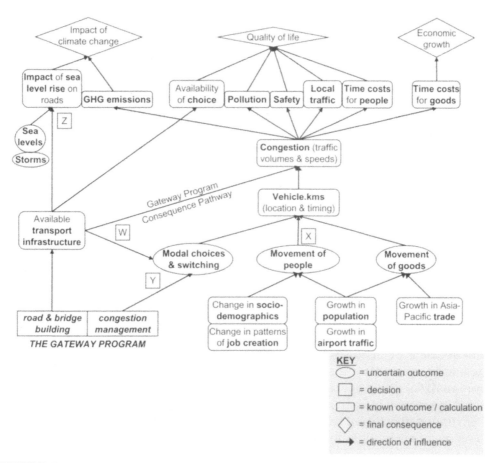

FIGURE 5 Influence diagram for the Gateway Programme (AMSD).

entailing multiple commutes; more school trips by car; an ageing population and midday driving. 'Change in patterns of job creation' refers to the impact that suburban business parks have had on traditional commuting patterns from suburbs to urban centres (BC Ministry of Transportation, 2006a). These and the other influences on overall demand are treated as exogenous parameters in the Gateway Programme documentation, and so are included as calculations or known outcomes. Finally, the Gateway Programme itself is shown in italics as the two decision nodes (rectangles) in the bottom left-hand corner, comprising road and bridge building and congestion management.

Figure 5 helps to emphasize various important points. The first is that the lack of influence of 'available transport infrastructure' (see box W in Figure 5) on 'movement of people' (see box X in Figure 5) reflects the reasoning behind the Gateway Programme that the demand for movement by road is a function of underlying socio-demographics and population rather than the availability of road infrastructure *per se*. While the Gateway Programme aims to affect people's choice of transport mode by encouraging HOV and non-vehicle modal choices (see box Y in Figure 5), its expected influence on overall demand (in vehicle.km) is less clear. The second point to note is that 'modal choices and switching' (see box Y in Figure 5) is the key determinant of whether the Gateway Programme achieves its objectives. Learning about the influence of the Gateway

Programme's new road infrastructure and congestion management measures on people's modal choices is therefore essential to evaluating its performance against its own stated objectives. 'Learning on mode-switching' could therefore serve as an intermediate node between the Gateway Programme and its final consequences, as well as a connection between initial and subsequent outcomes along a trajectory or consequence pathway, as suggested earlier in Figure 4. Finally, the inclusion of the climate change objectives on the left side of Figure 5 (see box Z in Figure 5) shows the influence of the road and bridge building component of the Gateway Programme on the exposure of the region's transportation infrastructure to the impacts of climate change (in this case, storms and sea-level rise). The low adaptability of infrastructure investments with long capital turnover cycles to future change (van Vliet et al., 2005) indicates the importance of considering these influences at the design phase of the Gateway Programme through, for example, storm water drainage or sea-level buffering.

4. Implementation issues

This article argues that structured decision-making tools (including objectives networks and influence diagrams) can help clarify linkages in AMSD decisions. The hope is that these methods can help in fostering transparency and stakeholder involvement, and thus contribute to creating more widely-supported, more adaptive, and better performing alternatives over time. However, whether these methods and tools are actually implemented to achieve these benefits is not straightforward. Here we discuss some experience with implementing structured decision-making approaches, and factors that can shape the extent and success of implementation.

Decision analysis as an operations research method has been increasingly applied and implemented in an array of contexts since the 1960s, ranging from medicine to energy planning, security, environmental issues, siting facilities and many others. Corner and Kirkwood (1991) provide a review of applications during 1970–1989, while Keefer et al. (2004) discuss applications from 1990 to 2001.

Structured decision-making as discussed in this article can be seen as building on formal decision analysis, but with an emphasis on stakeholder involvement for pluralistic decision processes rather than a single decision-maker. Applications of structured decision-making with stakeholders in public policy contexts are growing. The following are examples from the natural resource sector in British Columbia, Canada.

A series of decision-analytic, stakeholder-based advisory groups were remarkably successful in balancing economic, environmental and social objectives in water management for reservoir operations on 22 British Columbian river systems ((McDaniels et al., 1999; Gregory and Failing, 2002). This process was implemented in part because of regulatory pressures to find new approaches that could avoid litigation, build stakeholder support, and use values and technical information effectively to address conflict. An initial process on one river led to the development of guidelines for such processes and a province-wide series of water-use planning processes. Integrated resource planning at BC Gas was successfully conducted over two regulatory cycles with a structured decision process involving a stakeholder advisory group (Hobbs and Horne, 1997; Keeney and McDaniels, 1999). In this case, the impetus came from regulators seeking to improve the acceptability of the regulatory process.

Referendum design has also been influenced by decision-analytic concepts, in which stakeholders can choose among several alternatives for a policy decision (McDaniels, 1996; McDaniels and Thomas, 1999). Several other applications of structured decision-making for resource management issues in British Columbia are collated on a dedicated new website co-sponsored by the provincial government (www.structureddecisionmaking.org). Each application includes a discussion of why it arose, in what context, and how it provided support to a pluralistic decision process.

Practical applications of decision-analytic concepts to climate change adaptation or mitigation problems, however, are still rare. Ohlson (2005) applies decision-analytic approaches to park planning and fire mitigation under different climate change scenarios. Gregory and Failing (2002) have employed structured decision-making for water management decisions involving adaptation choices. Two further projects are under way in British Columbia to address climate adaptation in forest management decisions following pest infestations.

One reason for this slow adoption of structured decision-making approaches for climate change problems could simply be a lack of analysts familiar with decision-analytic practice as distinct from its theoretical basis. For example, there are few applications discussed in the UK CIP guide to climate adaptation (UK CIP, 2006), although the concepts of decision-making under uncertainty are discussed extensively.

It is also easy to understand some hesitancy with analytical methods that are conducted in conjunction with stakeholder processes. Managers and agencies may be concerned about time requirements, costs, and loss of control of the decision to be made. Yet experience suggests that the benefits of decisions that are better structured, more transparent, and widely supported, may outweigh the concerns over loss of control. Experience also suggests that structured decision processes may identify new alternatives that can provide substantial benefits at low costs or even with cost savings (Gregory and Failing, 2002).

Furthermore, this article also argues that even parts of a complete structured decision-making process can be highly beneficial and involve little cost or risk from the decision-maker's perspective. Influence diagrams and objectives networks can be developed in a few days of work, and can then serve as a basis for improving dialogue and understanding among all the parties to the decision. These methods can make tradeoffs more explicit and thus clearer and potentially manageable. The methods also can lead to the creation of better alternatives, even without extensive stakeholder consultation or formal advisory processes.

At the same time, we recognize that structured methods are not a panacea for overcoming differences in values or beliefs about impacts among stakeholders. The best that can be hoped for is better communication, which leads to shared understanding and a better framework within which difficult decisions for climate adaptation can be addressed.

5. Discussion

Many kinds of decisions are complex, in that they involve choice under uncertainty while balancing costs to achieve desired outcomes. Hence, attention to structured decision-making is widely important for human development and the wise use of limited resources (Hammond et al., 1999). AMSD decisions are particularly broad and complex, for many reasons noted earlier, and involve direct linkages in their objectives, alternatives and impacts. This article has demonstrated two approaches to structured decision-making: objectives networks, and influence diagrams. Both are useful heuristic approaches for decision support that can help address key characteristics of AMSD decisions: linkages across spatial and governance scales, linkages across timescales, multiple uncertainties, and the importance of learning over time.

While these approaches do not eliminate complexity, they do help to make AMSD linkages more tractable and easier to visualize. Hence interested parties will be more likely to understand the key issues in these decisions, and so be better equipped to contribute to analysis, discourse and implementation. All are necessary for effective AMSD choices.

Acknowledgements

The authors gratefully acknowledge the comments of two anonymous referees. The preparation of this article was supported by the Climate Decision Making Center (CDMC) at Carnegie Mellon University, through a cooperative agreement with the US National Science Foundation (SES-0345798), and through a sub-grant to the University of British Columbia.

Notes

1. These decisions will be dauntingly complex for myriad reasons, including: profound and irreducible uncertainties regarding the extent and pace of climate change to occur in the short and long term; conflicting values inherent in all environmental and technology choices that affect societal futures; behavioural, political and organizational responses to the changing environment that reinforce the status quo; the institutional and structural complexity of the decision-making environment (particularly the common property structure of climate change); and the long time horizons, high stakes and ethical issues, among others.
2. See, for example, the June 2007 Special Issue of *Mitigation and Adaptation Strategies for Global Change* 12(5) which addresses 'Challenges in Integrating Mitigation and Adaptation as Responses to Climate Change'.
3. Various writers have pointed out that adaptation decisions are typically made by entities such as individuals, organizations and governments, to address the impacts of climate change on them. Mitigation decisions are made by these same groups, within a public policy context, to reduce the rate and impacts of climate change globally. For the more significant adaptation decisions made by governments and organizations, some degree of stakeholder involvement drawn from civil society would be involved.
4. Many would argue that all such information is subjective, and thus subject to value influences, including technical questions. We agree. We also argue that it is possible to distinguish between information that is cast in terms of preferences, and that which relies on expertise, recognizing the importance of multiple perspectives in both domains.
5. Hammond et al. (1999) use the acronym PrOACT to capture these components: Problem, Objectives, Alternatives, Consequences, Tradeoffs.
6. Decision analysis has been applied to public policy decisions for decades. For example, Keeney and Raiffa (1993) include an application concerned with site selection for the Mexico City airport. Such analyses have generally been done for a client group rather than with the involvement of a broad group of stakeholders.
7. Another important tool used in structured decision-making is a consequence table, or an objectives by alternatives matrix (Hammond et al., 1999). While these tables appear deceptively simple, the process involved in creating them requires attention to the key steps of good decision process. Consequence tables have great power and salience as visual tools to clarify the pros and cons of alternatives, consider the tradeoffs that the alternatives offer, and think through preferred strategies. For examples, see Hammond et al. (1999) and MacRae and Whittington (1997).
8. Supplementary material on the Gateway Programme can be found at <www.gatewayprogram.bc.ca>.
9. We recognize that caution has been urged with regard to the ever-deeper integration of issues. Connecting everything in some way to everything else is not a useful decision aid (Ruth, 2005). However, the purpose of linking objectives using structured decision-making tools is to foster clarity, transparency, and shared understanding of policy goals and how different alternatives impact those goals. In particular, the inevitability of tradeoffs, once made clear, helps focus decision-makers on alternatives which either minimize adverse impacts on other agencies' objectives, or at least provide a clear basis for inter-agency negotiations towards integrated policies.
10. As an example, a performance criterion for the 'increase transport choices' objective might be '% of population living within 100 m of a cycle route' rather than '25% of population living within 100 m of a cycle route'.

References

Arthur, W.B., 1994, *Increasing Returns and Path Dependence in the Economy*, University of Michigan Press, Ann Arbor, MI.
Arvai, J., Gregory, R., McDaniels, T.L., 2001, 'Testing a structured decision approach: value-focused thinking for deliberative risk communication', *Risk Analysis* 21(6), 1065–1076.

Arvai, J., Bridge, G., Dolsak, N., Franzese, R., Koontz, T., Luginbuhl, A., Robbins, P., Richards, K., Korfmacher, S., Sohngen, B., Tansey, J., Thompson, A., 2006, 'Adaptive management of the global climate problem: bridging the gap between climate research and climate policy', *Climatic Change* 78(1), 217–225.

Bazerman, M., 2001, *Judgment in Managerial Decision Making*, Wiley, New York.

BC Ministry of Transportation, 2006a, *The Gateway Program: Program Definition Report*, BC Government, Victoria, BC, Canada.

BC Ministry of Transportation, 2006b, *Land Effects: Transportation and Land Use Linkages – A Literature Review*, BC Government, Victoria, BC, Canada.

Carmichael, J., Tansey, J., Robinson, J., 2004, 'An integrated assessment modeling tool', *Global Environmental Change* 14, 171–183.

Cash, D.W., Adger, W.N., Berkes, F., Garden, P., Lebel, L., Olsson, P., Pritchard, L., Young, O., 2006, 'Scale and cross-scale dynamics: governance and information in a multilevel world', *Ecology and Society* 11(2), 8 [available at www.ecologyandsociety.org/vol11/iss2/art8/].

Clemen, R.T., Reilly, T., 2001, *Making Hard Decisions*, Duxbury, Pacific Grove, CA.

Corner, J., Kirkwood, C., 1991, 'Decision analysis applications in the operations research literature', *Operations Research* 39(2), 206–219.

Dawes, R., 1988, *Rational Choice in an Uncertain World*, Harcourt Brace Jovanovich, San Diego, CA.

Dietz, T., Ostrom, E., Stern, P.C., 2003, 'The struggle to govern the commons', *Science* 302, 1907–1912.

Doherty, E., 2007, *Cooking the Books, Cooking the Planet: An Analysis of Gateway Greenhouse Gas Emissions Estimates*, Report prepared for SPEC (Society Promoting Environmental Conservation) [available at www.liveableregion.ca/pdf/Cooking_the_Books_Report_Final_05-02-07.pdf].

Fischhoff, B., 2006, 'Modeling: visualizing your vulnerabilities', *Harvard Business Review* May, 8–10.

Gregory, R., Failing, L., 2002, 'Using decision analysis to encourage sound deliberation: water use planning in British Columbia, Canada', *Journal of Policy Analysis and Management* 21(3), 492–499.

Gregory, R., Keeney, R.L., 1994, 'Creating policy alternatives using stakeholder values', *Management Science* 40(8), 1035–1048.

Gregory, R., Keeney, R.L., 2002, 'Making smarter environmental management decisions', *Journal of the American Water Resources Association* 36(6), 1601–1612.

Gunderson, L.H., Holling, C.S., 2002, *Panarchy: Understanding Transformations in Human and Natural Systems*, Island Press, Washington, DC.

Hammond, J., Keeney, R.L., Raiffa, H., 1999, *Smart Choices: A Practical Guide to Making Better Decisions*, Harvard Business School Press, Cambridge, MA.

Hobbs, B.F., Horne, G.T.F., 1997, 'Building public confidence in energy planning: a multimethod MCDM Approach to demand-side planning at BC Gas', *Energy Policy* 25(3), 357–375.

Holling, C.S., 1978, *Adaptive Environmental Assessment and Management*, John Wiley, Chichester, UK.

Howard, R. 1989, 'Knowledge maps', *Management Science* 35(8), 903–922.

Howard, R.A., Matheson., J.E. (eds), 1984, *Readings on the Principles and Applications of Decision Analysis*, Strategic Decisions Group, Menlo Park, CA.

IPCC, 2001, *Climate Change 2001: Mitigation. Contribution of Working Group III to the Third Assessment Report of the Intergovernmental Panel on Climate Change*, Cambridge University Press, Cambridge, UK.

Keefer, D.L., Kirkwood C.W., Corner, J.L., 2004, 'Perspective on decision analysis applications 1990–2001', *Decision Analysis* 1(1), 4–22.

Keeney, R.L., 1992, *Value-Focused Thinking: A Path to Creative Decision Making*, Harvard University Press, Cambridge, MA.

Keeney, R.L., Gregory, R., 2005, 'Selecting attributes to measure the achievement of objectives', *Operations Research* 53(1), 1–11.

Keeney, R.L., McDaniels, T.L., 1999, 'Identifying and structuring values to guide integrated resource planning at BC Gas', *Operations Research* 47(5), 651–661.

Keeney, R.L., McDaniels, T.L., 2001, 'A framework to guide thinking and analysis regarding climate change policies', *Risk Analysis* 21(6), 989–1000.

Keeney, R.L., Raiffa, H., 1993, *Decisions with Multiple Objectives: Preferences and Value Tradeoffs*, Cambridge University Press, Cambridge, UK.

MacPhee, I., Collins, B., Smith, M., 2006, *The Fraser Valley Light Rail: An Alternative to the Gateway Program*, Report prepared by Urban Studies, Simon Fraser University, Vancouver, BC, Canada.

MacRae, D., Whittington, D., 1997, *Expert Advice for Policy Choice*, Georgetown University Press, Washington, DC.

McDaniels, T., 1994, 'Sustainability, value tradeoffs and electric utility planning: a Canadian example', *Energy Policy* 22(12), 1045–1054.

McDaniels, T.L., 1996, 'The structured value referendum: eliciting preferences for environmental policy alternatives', *Journal of Policy Analysis and Management* 15(2), 227–251.

McDaniels, T.L., 2000, 'Creating and using objectives for ecological risk assessment and management', *Environmental Science and Policy* 3(6), 299–304.

McDaniels, T.L., Gregory, R., 2004, 'Learning as an objective within a structured risk management decision process', *Environmental Science and Technology* 38(7), 1921–1926.

McDaniels, T.L., Thomas, K., 1999, 'Eliciting public preferences for local land use alternatives: a structured value referendum with approval voting', *Journal of Policy Analysis and Management* 18(2), 264–280.

McDaniels, T.L., Gregory, R., Fields, D., 1999, 'Democratizing risk management: successful public involvement in local water management decisions', *Risk Analysis* 19(3), 497–510.

McDaniels, T.L., Dowlatabadi, H., Stevens, S., 2005, 'Multiple scales and regulatory gaps in environmental change: the case of salmon aquaculture', *Global Environmental Change* 15(1), 9–21.

McDaniels, T.L., Longstaff, H., Dowlatabadi, H., 2006, 'A value-based framework for risk management decisions involving multiple scales: a salmon aquaculture example', *Environmental Science and Policy* 49(4), 1–16.

Montgomery, C., 2006, 'Collision course: is Kevin Falcon's Gateway Program full of wrong turns?', *BC Business*, June 2006.

Morgan, M.G., Dowlatabadi, H., 1993, 'Learning from integrated assessment of climate change', *Climatic Change* 34, 3–4.

Morgan, M.G., Fischhoff, B., Bostrom, A., Atman, C.J., 2002, *Risk Communication: A Mental Models Approach*, Cambridge University Press, Cambridge, UK.

Ohlson, D., 2005, *Climate Change Adaptation Planning in British Columbia: A Case Study Investigation of Ecosystem Management in Mt. Robson Provincial Park*, Report for British Columbia Ministry of Environment, Victoria, BC, Canada.

Phillips, L.D., 1984, 'A theory of requisite decision models', *Acta Psychologica* 56, 29–48.

Renn, O., 2003, 'The challenge of integrating deliberation and expertise: participation and discourse in risk management', in: T.L. McDaniels, M. Small (eds), *Risk Analysis and Society: An Interdisciplinary Characterization of the Field*, Cambridge University Press, Cambridge, UK.

Robinson, J., 2003, 'Future Subjunctive: backcasting as social learning', *Futures* 35, 839–856.

Ruth, M., 2005, 'Future socio-economic and political challenges of global climate change', in: D. Pirages, K. Cousins (eds), *From Resource Scarcity to Ecological Security: Exploring New Limits to Growth*, The MIT Press, Cambridge, MA.

Shachter, R.D. 1986, 'Evaluating influence diagrams', *Operations Research* 34, 871–882.

Tansey, J., Carmichael, J., VanWynsberghe, R., Robinson, J., 2002, 'The future is not what it used to be: participatory integrated assessment in the Georgia Basin', *Global Environmental Change* 12(2), 97–104.

UK CIP, 2006, *Climate Impacts Programme* [available at www.ukcip.org.uk/resources/].

van Vliet, B., Chappells, H., Shove, E., 2005, *Infrastructures of Consumption: Environmental Innovation in the Utilities Industries*, Earthscan, London.

Willows, R., Connell, R., 2003, *Climate Adaptation: Risk, Uncertainty and Decision making*, UK Climate Impacts Programme, Technical Report, May 2003.

Wilson, C., Tansey, J., 2006, 'Integrating backcasting and decision analytic approaches to policy formulation: a conceptual framework', *Integrated Assessment* 6(4), 143–164.

Wilson, C., McDaniels, T.L., Bennett, R., 2006, 'What developers think about district energy: a mental models approach', in: *Proceedings of the 2006 ACEEE Summer Study on Energy Efficiency in Buildings*, American Council for an Energy Efficient Economy, Asilomar, CA.

■ outlook: insight

Integrating adaptation into policy: upscaling evidence from local to global

IAN BURTON[1], LIVIA BIZIKOVA[2]*, THEA DICKINSON[1], YVONNE HOWARD[1]

[1] Environment Canada, 4905 Dufferin Street, Downsview, Toronto, Ontario, M3H 5T4, Canada
[2] Adaptation and Impact Research Group (AIRG), Environment Canada and The Maurice Young Centre for Applied Ethics, The University of British Columbia, 6356 Agricultural Road, Vancouver, BC, V6T 1Z4, Canada

Historically, climate change has been viewed as an environmental pollution issue with international agreements narrowly focused on mitigation, while neglecting other responses including adaptation. This article discusses barriers and opportunities for the upscaling of adaptation into the international policy arena. It argues for the development of global adaptation models accounting for actual adaptation actions; for the refinement of processes that lead to adaptation; and for the accumulation of evidence from a growing number of adaptation case studies. A new challenge for adaptation science will be to integrate adaptation into the next phases of mitigation and development policy.

Keywords: adaptation; adaptation modelling; climate change; climate policy; international negotiations; policy formation; scale; sustainable development

Historiquement, le changement climatique a été considéré en terme de problème de pollution environnementale dont les accords internationaux sont étroitement centrés sur la mitigation, au défaut d'autres réponses telles que l'adaptation. Cet article débat des obstacles et possibilités de promotion de l'adaptation à l'intérieur de la sphère des politiques internationales. L'article est en faveur de l'expansion de modèles globaux d'adaptation incorporant les actions réelles, d'un raffinement des processus donnant lieu à l'adaptation, et à l'accumulation d'indices sur l'adaptation issus d'un nombre croissant d'études de cas sur l'adaptation. Un nouveau défi pour la science de l'adaptation sera d'intégrer l'adaptation dans les prochaines étapes des politiques de mitigation et de développement.

Mots clés: adaptation; changement du climat; développement durable; échelle; élaboration de politiques; modélisation de l'adaptation; négociations internationales; politique climatique

1. When does research drive policy and policy drive research?

It is widely understood that the research of atmospheric and environmental scientists placed climate change upon the global environmental agenda in the 1980s, driving the policy agenda (Burton et al., 2002). The policy process responded rapidly and the United Nations Framework Convention on Climate Change (UNFCCC) was negotiated in time for its signature at the UN Conference on Environment and Development (the 'Earth Summit') in Rio de Janeiro in 1992 (UN, 1992). The quickly negotiated Convention has yet to be proven effective.

The structure of the problem as formulated in the Convention was derived from atmospheric and environmental sciences (Corfee-Morlot and Agrawala, 2004). Climate change was viewed as an environmental problem for scientific analysis, while its human dimension was ignored (Cohen et al., 1998). Scientists cast the issue as a pollution problem and the Convention was conceived as a global-level pollution control instrument with the arbitrary response options being either 'mitigation' or 'adaptation'. In fact, adaptation was included only as an afterthought.

In seeking to be policy-relevant, subsequent research has followed the language and the structure of the Framework Convention. If the volume of adaptation and

■ * Corresponding author. *E-mail*: liviab@interchange.ubc.ca

© 2007 Earthscan ISSN: 1469-3062 (print), 1752-7457 (online) www.climatepolicy.com

mitigation research generated over the last 15 years had been available at the time of the negotiations on the Climate Convention, the underlying concept of the Convention may have been quite different and possibly taken longer to negotiate, but in the policy perspective, the UNFCCC was a case of 'seize the moment', with the deadline provided by the 'Earth Summit' bringing the negotiations to a speedy conclusion.

In the absence or delay of the Framework Convention, the history of research would also have been different, probably focusing on climate change as a problem in development and equity as well as environment. This article describes one view of how this set of circumstances came about and suggests policy implications from the research of the last 15 years. It also draws some anticipatory inferences for climate policy from the research that is now being proposed on the integration of adaptation and mitigation in the context of sustainable development.

2. The false structuring of the climate change issue?

Anthropogenic climate change was brought to public attention in the 1980s by atmospheric scientists. Improvements to weather forecasting by general circulation models (GCMs) were the motivation, where the models assumed a constant composition of the atmosphere. Atmospheric chemists called this assumption into question, noting the observation of increasing levels of carbon dioxide at the Mauna Loa site since 1959 (Keeling and Whorf, 2005). Subsequently, the models were updated and came to be called global climate models (GCMs). Within a short time, the models were producing dramatic scenarios, and the scientific evidence for human-induced climate change became more convincing.

These events followed rapidly on the heels of two other major atmospheric problems: acid precipitation and stratospheric ozone layer depletion (Oppenheimer and Petsonk, 2005). Eventually, after policy battles and scientific research, both problems were brought under control by the regulation of sulphur dioxide emissions and those of other harmful substances, including chlorofluorocarbons (CFCs). An important difference between the two problems was that of scale. The impacts of acid precipitation fell in the same region as the source of emissions. Therefore, while international cooperation was necessary, the problem could largely be managed on a continental scale (Clark et al., 2001). In the case of ozone layer depletion, the sources of CFC emissions and their effects were widespread at great distances from the source, especially at the southern polar regions (Moser and Dilling, 2007). The 'ozone hole' thus

became a matter for the UN, resulting in the 'Vienna Convention on Substances that Deplete the Ozone Layer' being negotiated in 1985, followed by the Montreal Protocol adopted in 1987.[1]

When climate change came to international attention, it was viewed as the third problem in a succession of atmospheric issues of growing complexity, but fundamentally of the same kind; and consequently was termed an environmental pollution problem (Clark et al., 2001). Article 2 of the Convention, in relation to any legal instruments,[2] emphasizes stabilizing concentrations of GHGs at a level that would prevent dangerous anthropogenic interference with the climate system within a time-frame sufficient to allow the natural adaptation of ecosystems, while ensuring food security and sustainable economic development (UN, 1992). The structure of the Article is modelled upon pollution control legislation (Yamin et al., 2006), which usually includes setting a general aspiration level of environmental contamination and listing criteria for the determination of specific levels at specific times. Since little was then known about the potential impacts of climate change, the language of the Article is lacking in the operational definition necessary to sufficiently guide adaptation and mitigation initiatives.

3. The growing influence of mitigation and adaptation research

Since 1992, there has been an explosion of research on the impacts of climate change, mitigation and adaptation. However, this research has not yet provided the scientific basis with which to answer the ambiguities generated by the Convention, although it does enable the necessary value judgements to be made in a more informed, insightful and enlightened way.[3] Much of the research has been captured and fed into the policy process by the successive reports of the Intergovernmental Panel on Climate Change (IPCC). This research has helped to bring forward the notion that climate change is more than a pollution problem with profound implications for the distribution of its impacts and responsibilities, especially in the case of mitigation, including both inter- and intra-generational dimensions (Beg et al., 2002). This awareness is helping to guide the negotiations towards the issues of equity and development (Eriksen and O'Brien, 2007) and these are becoming a larger component of the policy debates.

Another realization is that adapting to climate variability and climate extremes is not a new phenomenon; humanity has always been adapting to climate. The initial 'pollution' view of the climate-change issue led to a focus on mitigation. However, a pollution prevention or reduction strategy is a long-term process, and because of the lag times in the climate system, no mitigation effort (no matter how rigorous it is), is going to prevent climate change from happening in the next few decades (Pittock and Jones, 2000). The damage will continue to mount, impacting especially on the poorest of developing countries with a negligible contribution to the climate problem. Consequently a range of adaptation actions will be required before the stabilization of GHGs can be achieved.

However, the primary focus on mitigation created a view of adaptation as almost an opposite response from mitigation, to be employed only when mitigation fails to prevent impacts (Pielke, 2006). To a large extent, this underestimation of adaptation still persists. When adaptation is considered, unfortunately it is often merely to lament the lack of adaptive capacity in the poorest and most vulnerable communities and countries. Knowledge of past adaptation and research into the processes and techniques of adaptation still continue to be neglected.

With the emergence of atmospheric pollution issues, the focus of policy has shifted from local to global affairs, neglecting issues of community development (Ghersi et al., 2003; Wilbanks, 2007). Similarly, the Climate Convention promotes responses that have been negotiated at the supranational level, which may be seen as a powerful approach to address larger sources of GHGs, while possibly creating significant resources to support adaptation actions (i.e. a global adaptation fund to support the most vulnerable). However, at the international level, negotiators alone have limited power to reconcile diverse interests to promote significant actions. Effective responses to climate change should account for the local and regional situation, including encountered impacts, actual capacities and feasible responses. Strengthening the linkages between local, regional and global scales, by creating funds and initiatives, could assist in targeted place-based adaptation action (Jaeger et al., 2007; Swart and Raes, 2007) and help inject mitigation into development initiatives occurring on the ground.

The policy process still has some way to go before it fully integrates the issues raised by the research community on equity, development and the intractable nature of the greenhouse gas reduction problem. Policy-makers should acknowledge the fact that both mitigation and adaptation are a part of the portfolio of responses, and they will have to confront decisions about how to incorporate both types of response into a coherent and balanced strategy (Dang et al., 2003; Swart and Raes, 2007). In order to foster these types of actions, research has to take an interdisciplinary approach. Linkages need to be made between the socio-economic dimensions of impacts and responses, which would subsequently challenge institutional settings and potentially broaden policy-makers' dialogue.

4. AMSD research and the post-2012 regime

The climate negotiations are now at a critical phase. The end of the first commitment period under the Kyoto Protocol (2008–2012) is rapidly approaching. The negotiations are split into two tracks – the Kyoto track and the so-called 'Dialogue'. The Kyoto track consists of negotiations at the Meeting of the Parties to the Protocol (MOP; the USA is excluded), while the Dialogue takes place within the Conference of the Parties to the Convention (COP) with the involvement of the USA.

If significant progress is to be made by 2012 under either of these tracks, the issues of equity and development and the slow progress on mitigation and the potential for adaptation will have to be factored into the regime or agreement(s). Much of the current thinking is still mired in the false structures of the Convention dating from 1992. Extending the life of the Kyoto Protocol is still considered the first priority. The focus is on bringing the USA and big emitters in the developing world (China, India, Brazil and a few others) into the Protocol regime, even if this means changing the rules and the structure to accommodate their demands.[4] According to this mindset, the need to strengthen the adaptation regime and to incorporate (mainstream) climate risks into development is relegated to a second and lower priority. Therefore, attention (and financial assistance) may not be devoted to adaptation in the post-2012 regime unless (or until) agreement is reached on the mitigation agenda. However, the prospect of a successful outcome to the current phase of the climate negotiations cannot be rated as high.

The AMSD research proposed by the articles in this volume is a modest, but ambitious, attempt to make a different sort of contribution to the policy process while accounting for this complexity. It recognizes that whatever happens in the negotiations, actual solutions will have to be found on the ground, and these solutions will be more valuable if they can promote sustainable development while advancing both mitigation and adaptation.

In an optimistic perspective, it is possible to imagine a movement in the research community that would bring practical results and policy messages to communities and governments not only in Europe and North America, but also across the developing world. The programme of research and related activities envisaged here could be most helpful at the local level in terms of practical applications and at the national level in terms of policy. Is it possible that there might also be relevance for the Framework Convention itself and the post-2012 negotiations? This question brings us to the 'upscaling problem'.

5. Upscaling results to the global level

The research community has been developing a strong track record of locally based or site-specific research on adaptation. Research on mitigation, on the other hand, has mostly focused on methods of emission reduction, carbon sequestration, carbon capture and storage, including technology research and development, and research into regulatory and market mechanisms. Generally, none of these pursuits are site-specific.

If AMSD research is to have an impact beyond the local or national levels, it has to be 'upscaled' in order to be relevant to global negotiations. Two approaches are proposed. The first is in the field of adaptation modelling, which has received relatively little attention within the expanding field of integrated assessment modelling, in order to identify holistic patterns in which responses to climate change can be considered. The second approach is to allow the slowly accumulating evidence from local studies to permeate the negotiations. Just as adaptation research in the past has helped guide the negotiations towards greater emphasis on equity, development and adaptive capacity, so in the future could the combination of adaptation and mitigation studies at the local level gradually alter the mindset of the negotiators. It is doubtful whether this can happen quickly enough to significantly influence the negotiations on the post-2012 regime. But the mere fact that this new generation of research is under way could spur some movement towards a broader and more balanced approach to the post-2012 strategy.

Possibilities that have been suggested for the post-2012 regime include more emphasis on adaptation in a form of a separate legal instrument for adaptation (LIFA), or a revised and expanded Kyoto Protocol. The content of such an adaptation framework might include mandated (as opposed to voluntary) funding for adaptation linked to national adaptation plans of action in developing, and potentially all, countries. The distribution of resources could be facilitated by the Convention, and could be supported by insurance products delivered through public–private arrangements. Such developments would strengthen adaptation, but would not necessarily integrate it with mitigation; consequently, a higher dependence on fossil fuels may be perpetuated. To avoid this outcome, not only would co-benefits and synergies have to be demonstrated (e.g. by some examples as in the case of AMSD studies: Eriksen and O'Brien, 2007; Ruth and Coelho, 2007), but a system of trade-offs would need to be established; one example would be the implementation of a system of voluntary or involuntary offset charges on GHG-generating adaptations.

The faster local-scale research on adaptation, mitigation and sustainable development can be extended, and the sooner the case study evidence begins to mount, the better the chances of a truly effective post-2012 regime.

6. Adaptation modelling

Climate models have evolved by combining GCMs with global energy models into 'integrated assessment models' (IAMs). The development of IAMs has proceeded without much serious attempt to incorporate adaptation. A recent salient example is the modelling work that underlies the Stern Review, in which calamitous consequences of climate change are predicted in the absence of much stronger mitigation actions, but with little recognition of the potential power of adaptation (Stern, 2007).

The benefits of including adaptation in IAMs would be substantial. At present, when adaptation *is* considered in integrated assessments, it is commonly as an attempt to answer the question 'how much can adaptation reduce impacts?' The resultant 'models' (in the broadest sense of the term) enable decision-makers to assess the merits of particular adaptation choices – for example the UKCIP tool 'Adaptation Wizard' (UKCIP, 2005) and the 'Community-based Risk Screening Tool' (IISD, 2006). These are essentially adaptation support or decision support tools rather than adaptation models.

Such tools provide no insight into the actual adaptation process itself; they rely on the capacity of decision-makers to create the channels and deliver the actions (for some examples, see Wilson and McDaniels, 2007). Thus, if the objective is to understand how best to promote and facilitate adaptation, then the models needed are of the adaptation process. It is therefore intended that the case studies in the AMSD project will highlight the need for adaptation models that work in conjunction with mitigation modelling. First steps in this direction can be the recognition of shared capacities needed for both adaptation and mitigation (Burch and Robinson, 2007). To the extent that adaptation can be incorporated with mitigation and IAMs, there is potential for the 'scaling up' of adaptation to the global policy level.

7. Accumulating the case study evidence

The second approach to 'upscaling' is simply to accumulate evidence from the growing number of adaptation case studies. Although such locality-specific research can be difficult to categorize, a number of strategies can be used to improve the prospects for comparability (AAG, 2003).

In addition, the great variety of circumstances offers an opportunity for learning more about causes, consequences, and alternative strategies at a local scale (Wilbanks, 2003).

This type of examination is currently being attempted in Canada through a national assessment of impacts and adaptations (Lemmen and Warren, 2005). The project is uncovering a rich array of anecdotal examples of past, current and potential future adaptation measures. By comparing and contrasting adaptations in this manner, the adaptation process should move along more rapidly. As climate change adaptations across sectors are recognized, it is more likely that other individuals, communities and industries will begin the process of adaptation as well.

Nonetheless, the aggregation of this information into some generic form that will guide the adaptation process is problematic. The mitigation agenda has so readily infiltrated public policy thus far because it can be simplified to a common currency – the emission of GHGs – around which targets can be based. However, adaptation options cover such a broad spectrum of costs and benefits that the definition of a common currency is far more ambiguous, if not impossible. Mainstreaming adaptation into climate change strategy will require a method for comparing the costs and benefits, or effectively determining the real size of an investment, for different adaptation options. Case studies could help with this task by establishing which types of adaptations are most appealing, how much decision-makers are currently willing to invest, and the level of scientific certainty they require.

The Global Environment Facility (GEF) (sponsored Assessments of Impacts and Adaptations to Climate Change (AIACC) project), is a global initiative developed to advance understanding of vulnerabilities and adaptation options in developing countries, which has generated a rich array of examples (START, 2006). The task of drawing general conclusions internationally faces the same difficulties as those experienced in Canada. In a draft paper (I. Burton et al., unpublished), a list of nine lessons has been drawn from the AIACC case studies. These have been stated as:

- Adapt now!
- Adaptation *is* development
- Adaptation is for ourselves
- International financial help is necessary
- Strengthen institutions
- Involve those at risk
- Use sector-based approaches
- Expand information, awareness and technical knowledge
- Adaptation is place-based (Burton et al., 2006).

8. Integrating adaptation and mitigation in models and case studies

The objective of AMSD is to create a greater understanding of the potential for managing the climate change issue through a combination of adaptation and mitigation measures. If this can be done in a manner that also facilitates or achieves a degree of 'upscaling', there is some prospect that the 'pollution squint' of the UNFCCC can be further modified, and that the difficult path selected in 1992 could be expanded in such a way that it produces greater benefits locally, nationally and globally.

A second reason for optimism is the growth of a regional approach to mitigation by the development of carbon markets, and trading regimes in Europe and parts of the USA. The obstacles encountered at the global level may prove to be tractable at the regional level, and it is possible that a number of other regional carbon markets will develop in other regions. A challenge for adaptation science, and for projects like AMSD, is to find ways of incorporating adaptation into the next advances in mitigation and development policy and perhaps enhancing the capacities needed to respond to climate change. We are setting out on an uncharted path and the prospects are both challenging and exciting.

Notes

1. The Montreal Protocol (1987) finally entered into force on 1 January 1989.
2. It is possible that the idea of a protocol modelled on the Montreal Protocol was already in circulation.
3. The European Union has been emboldened to specify 'plus 2 degrees Celsius above pre-industrial levels' as the threshold of 'dangerous' (Schellnhuber et al., 2006). It is a critical level that has not been universally accepted, even though it is gaining visibility, perhaps because it has the advantages of clarity.
4. This discussion is largely on hold in the hope that the next US presidential election will bring to office a more sympathetic administration.

References

AAG (Association of American Geographers), 2003, *Global Change in Local Places: Estimating, Understanding, and Reducing Greenhouse Gases*, GCLP Research Team, Association of American Geographers, Cambridge University Press, Cambridge, UK.

Beg, N., Corfee-Morlot, J., Davidson, O., Afrane-Okesse, Y., Tyani, L., Denton, F., Sokona, Y., Thomas, J.P., La

Rovere, E.L., Parikh, J.K., Parikh, K., Atiq Rahman, A., 2002, 'Linkages between climate change and sustainable development', *Climate Policy* 2, 129–144.

Burch, S., Robinson, J., 2007, 'A framework for explaining the links between capacity and action in response to global climate change', *Climate Policy* 7(4), 304–316.

Burton, I., Huq, S., Lim, B., Pilifosova, O., Schipper, E.L., 2002, 'From impacts assessment to adaptation priorities: the shaping of adaptation policy', *Climate Policy* 2, 145–159.

Burton, I., Diringer, E., Smith, J., 2006, *Adaptation to Climate Change: International Policy Options*, Pew Center on Global Climate Change, Arlington, VA.

Clark, W.C., Jäger, J., van Eijndhoven, J., Dickson, N.M., 2001, *Learning to Manage Global Environmental Risks. Volume 1: A Comparative History of Social Responses to Climate Change, Ozone Depletion, and Acid Rain*, The Social Learning Group, MIT Press, Cambridge, MA.

Cohen, S., Demeritt, D., Robinson, J., Rothman, D., 1998, 'Climate change and sustainable development: towards dialogue', *Global Environmental Change* 8, 341–371.

Corfee-Morlot, J., Agrawala, S., 2004, 'The benefits of climate policy', *Global Environmental Change* 14, 197–199.

Dang, H.H., Michaelowa, A., Tuan D.D., 2003, 'Synergy of adaptation and mitigation strategies in the context of sustainable development: the case of Vietnam', *Climate Policy* 3(S1), S81–S96.

Eriksen, S.H., O'Brien, K., 2007, 'Vulnerability, poverty and the need for sustainable adaptation measures', *Climate Policy* 7(4), 337–352.

Ghersi, F., Hourcade, J.-C., Criqui, P., 2003, 'Viable responses to the equity–responsibility dilemma: a consequentialist view', *Climate Policy* 3(S1), S115–S133.

IISD, 2006, *Crystal Tool, Community-based Risk Screening Tool: Livelihoods and Adaptation*, IISD, Winnipeg, Canada.

Jaeger, C.C., Hasselmann, K., Johannesen, O., Haas, A., Gallehr, S., Battaglini, A., Loh, C., Sprinz, D., 2007, *Meeting the Climate Challenge: The Need for Regional Climate Funds*, Potsdam Institute for Climate Impact Research, Potsdam, Germany.

Keeling, C.D., Whorf, T.P., 2005, *Atmospheric Carbon Dioxide Record from Manna Loa*, Carbon Dioxide Research Group, Scripps Institution of Oceanography, University of California, La Jolla, CA.

Lemmen, D.S., Warren, F.J. (eds), 2005, *Climate Change Impacts and Adaptation: A Canadian Perspective*, Natural Resources Canada, Ottawa, Canada.

Montreal Protocol, 1987, *Evolution of the Montreal Protocol*, United National Environment Programme, Ozone Secretariat [available at http://ozone.unep.org/Treaties_and_Ratification/2B_montreal_protocol.shtml].

Moser, S.C., Dilling, L. (eds), 2007, *Creating a Climate for Change*, Cambridge University Press, Cambridge, UK.

Oppenheimer, M., Petsonk, A., 2005, 'Article 2 of the UNFCCC: historical origins, recent interpretations', *Climatic Change* 73, 195–226.

Pielke, R.A., Jr, 2006, 'Misdefining "climate change": consequences for science and action', *Environmental Science and Policy* 8, 548–561.

Pittock, A.B., Jones, R.N., 2000. 'Adaptation to what and why?', *Environmental Monitoring and Assessment* 61, 9–35.

Ruth, M., Coelho, D., 2007, 'Understanding and managing the complexity of urban systems under climate change', *Climate Policy* 7(4), 317–336.

Schellnhuber, H.J., Cramer, W., Nakicenovic, N., Wigley, T., Yohe, G. (eds), 2006, *Avoiding Dangerous Climate Change*, Cambridge University Press, Cambridge, UK [available at www.defra.gov.uk/environment/climate change/research/dangerous-cc/index.htm].

START, 2006, *Assessments of Impacts and Adaptation to Climate Change (AIACC)* [available at www.start.org/Program/AIACC.html].

Stern, N., 2007, *The Economics of Climate Change: The Stern Review*, Cambridge University Press, Cambridge, UK.

Swart, R., Raes, F., 2007, 'Making integration of adaptation and mitigation work: mainstreaming into sustainable development policies?' *Climate Policy* 7(4), 288–303.

UKCIP, 2005, *UKCIP Tools: Adaptation Wizard* [available at www.ukcip.org.uk/resources/tools/adapt.asp].

UN (United Nations), 1992, *United Nations Framework Convention on Climate Change*, FCCC/Informal/84 GE.05-62220 (E) 200715 [available at http://unfccc.int/resource/docs/convkp/conveng.pdf].

Wilbanks, T.J., 2003, 'Integrating mitigation and adaptation as possible responses to global climate change', *Environment* 45, 28–38.

Wilbanks, T.J., 2007, 'Scale and sustainability', *Climate Policy* 7(4), 278–287.

Wilson, C., McDaniels, T., 2007, 'Structured decision-making to link climate change and sustainable development', *Climate Policy* 7(4), 353–370.

Yamin, F., Smith, J.B., Burton, I., 2006, 'Perspectives on "Dangerous Anthropogenic Interference"; or how to operationalize Article 2 of the UN Framework Convention on Climate Change', in: H.J. Schellnhuber, W. Cramer, N. Nakicenovic, T. Wigley, G. Yohe (eds), *Avoiding Dangerous Climate Change*, Cambridge University Press, Cambridge, UK, 81–91.

*For Product Safety Concerns and Information please contact
our EU representative GPSR@taylorandfrancis.com Taylor & Francis
Verlag GmbH, Kaufingerstraße 24, 80331 München, Germany*

T - #0203 - 270225 - C0 - 262/190/6 - PB - 9781138012219 - Gloss Lamination